Introduction

1 Spot the mistakes
1 swiming: swimming, weid: wide,
2 Gess: Guess, price: prize,
3 no: know, diep: deep,
4 forgett: forget, geare: gear,
5 conzert: concert, awsome: awesome

2 More about ... The Grand Canyon Skywalk
1 kind, *2* steel, *3* through, *4* take,
5 visitors, *6* pay, *7* expensive, *8* build

3 Words in pictures: outdoor activities
1 boots – hiking
2 saddle – riding
3 paddle – canoeing / paddling
4 swimming trunks / swimsuit – swimming
5 bike – cycling
6 tent – camping
7 skis – skiing
8 running shoes – running
9 skateboard – skating
10 racket – tennis

4 Lost words
1 in, *2* on, *3* along, *4* in, *5* to,
6 at/at, *7* in, *8* at, *9* to, *10* without

5 The best word
1 daily, *2* awesome, *3* busy,
4 whole, *5* lucky, *6* national,
7 deep, *8* natural

6 German-English crossword

7 Last letter – first letter
1 comment, *2* tent, *3* tool,
4 listener, *5* rim, *6* monument,
7 teach, *8* hike, *9* enough,
10 human, *11* natural

8 Odd word out
1 grade, *2* toes, *3* comment, *4* awful,
5 bed, *6* human, *7* wing, *8* deep,
9 forgive, *10* daily

9 Word search

K	W	U	C	G	K	A	E	A	A	F	U	P
U	O	S	A	E	R	K	Q	S	W	I	M	J
M	O	U	N	T	A	I	N	B	F	E	X	L
C	D	E	O	Y	P	T	G	V	M	L	W	H
O	S	X	E	O	I	S	L	A	N	D	V	F
U	P	C	E	U	D	O	K	L	D	X	D	X
N	F	O	R	E	S	T	M	L	L	J	L	S
T	N	A	O	S	D	P	B	E	A	C	H	G
R	M	S	D	N	H	G	R	Y	Q	J	I	A
Y	M	T	R	T	I	U	Q	T	L	N	K	M
S	T	M	I	V	L	F	M	H	U	S	E	A
I	K	O	V	U	L	W	Y	C	B	K	X	J
D	I	K	E	V	V	G	L	O	L	I	M	X
E	Q	H	R	O	C	K	B	B	T	X	P	S

swim – schwimmen, **mountain** – Berg,
island – Insel, **forest** – Wald,
beach – Strand, **sea** – Meer,
rock – Felsen, **countryside** – Landschaft, Natur,
woods – Wald, **coast** – Küste,
canoe – Kanu, **river** – Fluss,
rapids – Stromschnellen, **hill** – Hügel,
valley – Tal, **field** – Feld,
ski – Ski laufen, **hike** – wandern

Unit 1

1 Scrambled words: American and British English

1 grade, class
2 gas, petrol
3 gas station, petrol station
4 line, queue
5 downtown, city centre
6 auto, car
7 sidewalk, pavement
8 awesome, excellent
9 license plate, number plate

2 Number crossword

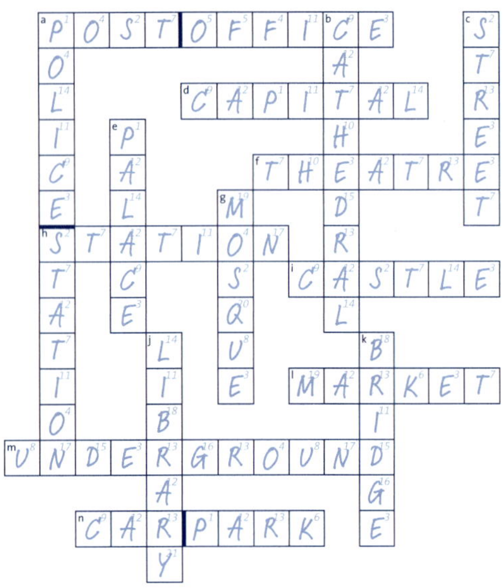

Brücke – **k** down
Markt – **l** across
Hauptstadt – **d** across
Bahnhof – **h** across
Postamt – **a** across
Moschee – **g** down
Palast – **e** down
Schloss – **i** across
Bibliothek – **j** down
U-Bahn – **m** across
Polizeiwache – **a** down
Parkplatz – **n** across

3 Verb forms

1 lie – lay – lain
2 forgive – forgave – forgiven
3 catch – caught – caught
4 hide – hid – hidden
5 meet – met – met
6 ride – rode – ridden
7 put – put – put
8 feel – felt – felt
9 forget – forgot – forgotten
10 take – took – taken
11 wear – wore – worn
12 feed – fed– fed
13 sing – sang – sung
14 drink – drank – drunk
15 tell – told – told
16 lose – lost – lost

4 Words in pictures

1 helmets, baseball caps
2 bank robbers, fish
3 buildings, clothes
4 instruments, football
5 cameras, microphones

5 What are the words?

1 somebody else, *2* where else,
3 something else, *4* nobody else,
5 What else, *6* everywhere else,
7 everybody else, *8* Who else

6 Last letter – first letter

1 queue, *2* end, *3* deli,
4 immigrant, *5* tip, *6* pavement,
7 thousand, *8* directions, *9* stop,
10 poor, *11* rich, *12* first,
13 route

7 Hidden words

1 nose, *2* note, *3* fine, *4* sofa,
5 train, *6* toast, *7* rain, *8* stone,
9 neat, *10* often, *11* trainers

8 More about ... Remembering 9/11

1 you, *2* touch, *3* near,
4 work, *5* on, *6* whole,
7 who, *8* where

9 Hour glasses

1		A	S	K	
2	H	I	K	E	S
3	R	O	Y	A	L
4	U	P	S	E	T
5		I	C	E	
			R		
6		M	A	P	
7	P	A	P	E	R
8	C	R	E	A	M
9	M	A	R	C	H
10		U	S	E	

1		O	F	F	
2	D	A	I	L	Y
3	L	A	R	G	E
4	C	L	E	A	N
5		O	F	F	
			I		
6		A	G	E	
7	O	T	H	E	R
8	E	N	T	E	R
9	F	I	E	L	D
10		A	R	T	

Das geheime Wort lautet:
Englisch – firefighter,
Deutsch – Feuerwehrmann/-frau

10 Odd word out

1 pavement, *2* downtown, *3* short, *4* bank, *5* bed, *6* sad, *7* queue, *8* fire station, *9* counter, *10* bagel

11 Spot the mistakes

1 sycle: cycle, pavment: pavement,
2 poeple: people, queu: queue,
3 perfekt: perfect, picknick: picnic,
4 vew: view, flor: floor,
5 els: else, evrything: everything

12 Word search

B	I	S	C	U	I	T	X	S	S	Q	U	T	K	T
A	T	H	R	O	H	B	P	C	A	R	R	O	T	U
G	W	T	E	A	F	A	P	P	L	E	E	M	X	R
E	A	Q	A	J	J	V	O	G	M	E	H	A	Y	K
L	M	K	M	K	U	H	R	S	O	W	H	T	P	E
V	A	N	C	H	I	C	K	E	N	K	W	O	U	Y
G	T	P	H	J	C	I	G	L	H	J	A	O	Y	X
C	H	E	E	S	E	J	T	O	A	S	T	P	P	M
O	X	R	E	N	V	B	J	Q	T	M	E	N	W	U
F	C	A	S	T	R	A	W	B	E	R	R	Y	H	S
F	O	P	E	D	O	C	H	U	V	S	H	S	B	H
E	M	R	T	M	X	O	W	T	U	C	A	K	E	R
E	Q	O	N	I	O	N	W	T	U	O	A	Q	E	O
D	V	L	P	M	Y	O	V	E	P	L	B	S	F	O
H	L	L	A	M	B	J	B	R	E	A	D	A	O	M

Fruit and vegetables
carrot – Möhre, apple – Apfel, strawberry – Erdbeere, onion – Zwiebel, tomato – Tomate, mushroom – Pilz
Drinks
tea – Tee, coffee – Kaffee, juice – Saft, cola – Cola, water – Wasser
Milk products
cream cheese – Frischkäse, cheese – Käse, butter – Butter
Bread, cake, etc.
bagel – Bagel, biscuit – Keks, toast – Toast(brot), cake – Kuchen, bread – Brot, roll – Brötchen
Meat and fish
chicken – Huhn, lamb – Lammfleisch, bacon – Schinkenspeck, pork – Schweinefleisch, salmon – Lachs, beef – Rindfleisch, turkey – Truthahn/Pute

13 Words with different meanings

1 **line** – Zeile/Schlange
2 **cross** – überqueren/sauer
3 **tall** – hohes (Gebäude)/groß
4 **tip** – Spitze/Tipp
5 **break** – Pause/kaputt machen
6 **floor** – Boden/Stock

14 Pronunciation

eɪ – grade, pavement, sale, take
æ – avenue, gas, hijacker, map
ə – breakfast, admission, dollar, forward
ɑː – apartment, grass, path, start
ɔː – also, call, awesome, sidewalk

15 The fourth word

1 collection, *2* wings, *3* foot, *4* dollar, *5* mile, *6* long, *7* first floor, *8* below, *9* middle school, *10* burn, *11* petrol station/gas station, *12* ticket office, *13* fish, *14* dish, *15* firefighter, *16* sale

16 Word friends

take: a break, notes, a photo
kick: the ball, a dog, another player
burn: old clothes, a newspaper, wood
take over: a plane, a bank, a company
earn: good money, a lot, $10 an hour

17 Word ladder
ride – side – hide – hike – like – line – fine – find – kind – king – wing – wind – mind – mine – mile – mole – more – sore – some – same – sale – **salt**

18 Lost words
1 of, *2* to, *3* out, *4* out,
5 in, *6* on, *7* of

19 Word groups
places to eat or drink
juice bar, café, canteen, deli, pub, restaurant
money
cent, dollar, euro, pence, penny, pound
roads and paths:
cycle path, avenue, highway, pavement, road, route, street
jobs
waiter, editor, firefighter, musician, policeman, ranger, waitress

Unit 2

1 Words in pictures
1 kiss, *2* scream, *3* shout,
4 cry, *5* whisper, *6* explain

2 Odd word out
1 dinosaur, *2* safety, *3* earn,
4 blood, *5* cry, *6* zoo, *7* a pair,
8 beard, *9* false, *10* earth

3 Word search

C	A	T	H	E	D	R	A	L	X	B	U	S	J	N	U	M
S	B	R	O	C	H	U	R	E	W	O	E	J	M	A	B	O
I	R	P	L	A	N	E	B	B	B	A	M	I	X	T	A	T
M	B	F	X	U	M	M	T	I	E	T	E	N	T	I	C	E
O	A	V	A	X	O	U	V	K	D	N	P	A	R	O	K	L
H	Y	N	Q	G	S	G	U	E	&	H	I	Y	A	N	P	K
O	S	J	Y	N	Q	W	C	A	B	I	N	V	I	A	A	R
L	S	J	H	D	U	F	C	A	R	A	V	A	N	L	C	U
I	U	H	O	T	E	L	Q	E	E	W	S	A	B	P	K	C
D	I	X	B	Y	C	H	C	L	A	Y	C	R	R	A	G	K
A	T	H	S	M	V	Q	A	R	K	C	A	D	J	R	L	S
Y	C	O	Q	U	X	F	S	M	F	E	R	R	Y	K	L	A
F	A	S	U	S	D	E	T	K	A	N	Q	Q	D	D	Y	C
L	S	T	C	E	I	H	L	G	S	H	I	P	U	F	I	K
A	E	E	N	U	T	E	E	A	T	I	C	K	E	T	S	X
T	U	L	O	M	O	N	U	M	E	N	T	M	M	M	A	P

4 Definitions
1 leaves – live: immigrant
2 tall – apartments: skyscraper
3 line – cars: queue
4 wait – fire: fire station
5 side – walk: pavement
6 planes – fly: wings

5 Scrambled words: On a farm
1 cut, *2* prepare, *3* keep, *4* feed,
5 look after, *6* produce, *7* grow, *8* use,
9 sell, *10* kill, *11* pack, *12* make

6 Spot the mistakes
1 your: you're, brake: break
2 wein: wine, there: their
3 Gait: Gate, attraktion: attraction
4 creme: cream, koffee: coffee
5 by: buy, produkts: products

7 Word families
1 drawing, *2* production,
3 kiss, *4* argument,
5 success, *6* attack,
7 spelling, *8* hike,
9 revision, *10* plant,
11 translate, *12* discriminate

8 Last letter – first letter
1 grab, *2* belong, *3* grape,
4 ethnic, *5* cheek, *6* kiss,
7 short, *8* tall, *9* laugh,
10 homeless, *11* safety,
12 yard, *13* disadvantage

9 Opposites
1 dark, *2* safe, *3* short, *4* minority,
5 disadvantage, *6* put out, *7* below,
8 most, *9* good at, *10* lose

10 More about ... Los Angeles
1 know, *2* live, *3* largest, *4* size,
5 main, *6* other, *7* capital, *8* too

11 Synonyms
1 afraid/scared, *2* big/large,
3 call/phone, *4* opinion/view,
5 difficult/hard, *6* begin/start,
7 journey/trip, *8* boat/ship,
9 field/pitch, *10* above/over

12 Word ladder
cook – book – look – lock – sock – sick – kick – pick – pack – back – bank – band – land – lane – line – wine – wind – **wild**

13 Crossword
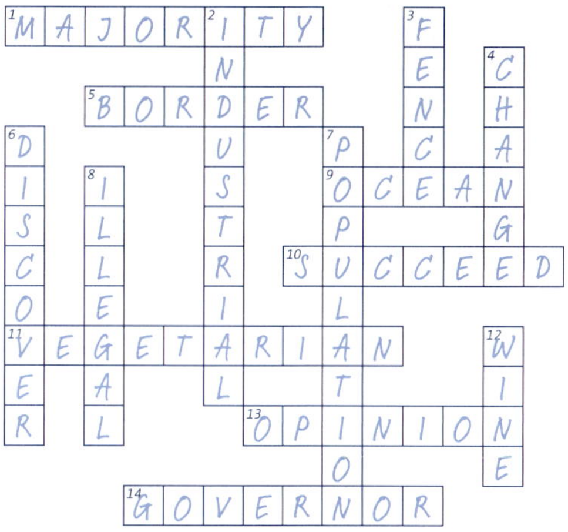

14 The best word
1 perfect, *2* endless, *3* industrial, *4* legal, *5* specific, *6* social

15 Words with different meanings
1 act – verhalten/spielen,
2 pretty – ziemlich/hübsche (Frau),
3 right – richtig/rechts,
4 change – umsteigen/ändere,
5 work out – herauszufinden/gut ausgehen,
6 hard – heftig/schwer,
7 little – kleine (Hütte)/wenig (Zeit)

16 Hour glasses

1		A	S	K	
2	T	O	P	I	C
3	B	L	O	N	D
4	B	O	R	E	D
5		A	T	E	
			S		
6		O	W	N	
7	S	H	O	R	T
8	W	O	M	A	N
9	G	R	A	P	E
10		E	N	D	

1		A	C	T	
2	B	L	O	C	K
3	H	U	M	A	N
4	O	F	F	E	R
5		Z	O	O	
			R		
6		A	T	E	
7	C	R	A	S	H
8	C	A	B	I	N
9	R	E	L	A	X
10		F	E	W	

Das geheime Wort lautet:
Englisch – comfortable,
Deutsch – bequem

17 Lost words
1 to, *2* against, *3* for, *4* in, *5* up, *6* into, *7* against, *8* in, *9* of, *10* over

18 Word pairs
beg for – help, belong to – club, change – plans, cost – $50, cut – grass, discover – planet, get to know – people, give up – smoking, kick – ball, kiss – cheek, press – button, put out – fire, take – break

Unit 3

1 Word search

M	Y	C	J	I	G	O	D	Y	D	S	O	N
O	U	O	M	U	R	C	U	O	Y	S	H	I
T	X	U	D	T	A	D	F	G	W	I	F	E
H	U	S	B	A	N	D	P	C	S	T	V	C
E	F	I	T	T	D	X	Y	U	N	C	L	E
R	S	N	X	Y	P	T	J	G	T	H	B	H
O	Y	I	G	R	A	N	D	C	H	I	L	D
T	R	P	T	U	R	R	T	O	K	L	M	A
R	N	E	P	H	E	W	S	S	F	D	U	U
T	I	D	A	X	N	A	S	V	C	C	Q	G
W	A	B	R	O	T	H	E	R	Y	W	Q	H
I	I	R	E	V	S	P	G	H	A	U	N	T
N	I	B	N	E	B	J	C	Y	J	O	F	E
S	I	S	T	E	R	F	F	A	T	H	E	R
G	B	D	S	L	K	X	J	N	G	L	Q	O

son – Sohn
wife – Ehefrau
husband – Ehemann
uncle – Onkel
grandchild – Enkel/in
nephew – Neffe
brother – Bruder
aunt – Tante
sister – Schwester
father – Vater
mother – Mutter
twins – Zwillinge
cousin – Cousin, Cousine
parents – Eltern
grandparents – Großeltern
child – Kind
niece – Nichte
daughter – Tochter

2 Scrambled Words: School
1 classroom, *2* revise, *3* exchange, *4* explain, *5* project, *6* lesson, *7* essay, *8* head, *9* exercise, *10* look up, *11* board, *12* subject

3 Last letter – first letter
1 jacket, *2* trainers, *3* sweatshirt, *4* top, *5* pyjamas, *6* shirt, *7* trousers, *8* shorts, *9* skirt, *10* tights, *11* socks, *12* shoes

4 Verb forms
1 make – made – made
2 begin – began – begun
3 tear – tore – torn
4 study – studied – studied
5 cry – cried – cried
6 shake – shook – shaken
7 take – took – taken
8 keep – kept – kept
9 run – ran – run
10 break – broke – broken

5 The fourth word
1 men, *2* feet, *3* thieves, *4* wolves, *5* potatoes, *6* child, *7* tooth, *8* wife, *9* mouse, *10* quiz

6 Hidden words
1 read, *2* tree, *3* knee, *4* Greek, *5* king, *6* earring, *7* green, *8* drink, *9* ride, *10* tiger, *11* great

7 What are the words?
1 (sich) verändern
2 wechseln
3 (sich) umziehen
4 umsteigen
5 wechseln

8 Spot the mistakes
1 want: wants, studie: study
2 reis: rice, meel: meal
3 hole: whole, meating: meeting
4 whole: hole, schuh: shoe
5 brake: break, troble: trouble
6 debatte: debate, klass: class
7 exersise: exercise, frish: fresh
8 forein: foreign, countrys: countries

9 Pronunciation
aɪ – fight, alive, countryside, exercise, light, wine
ɪ – sick, bulletin, engine, kindergarten, meeting, tradition
iː – magazine, kilo, machine, pizza, police, ski

10 Lost words
1 at, *2* in, *3* at, *4* at/at, *5* for, *6* in, *7* for, *8* on, *9* on

11 More about...German immigrants in North America
1 millions, *2* first, *3* number, *4* went, *5* in, *6* newspapers, *7* Jewish, *8* escape, *9* as, *10* families

12 Definitions
1 school – between: **kindergarten**
2 thing – country: **foreign**
3 come – decide: **meeting**
4 activities – lessons: **extracurriculars**
5 take – different: **change**

13 Word ladder
dark – mark – park – pork – work – word – wore – sore – some –same – sale – male – mile – mice – rice – ride – **hide**

14 Word friends
1 **break** the window, a plate, the rules
2 **found** a school, a company, a club
3 **summarize** a story, a play, information
4 **get involved** in a club, in a football team, in a school newspaper
5 **belong to** a minority, the majority, a club
6 **elect** a leader, a new parliament, a government
7 **beg for** something to eat, money, help

15 Word building
1 boyfriend, *2* girlfriend, *3* dress code, *4* sportswoman, *5* sparkling water, *6* sister city, *7* hometown, *8* traffic light, *9* ticket office, *10* firefighter

16 Number crossword
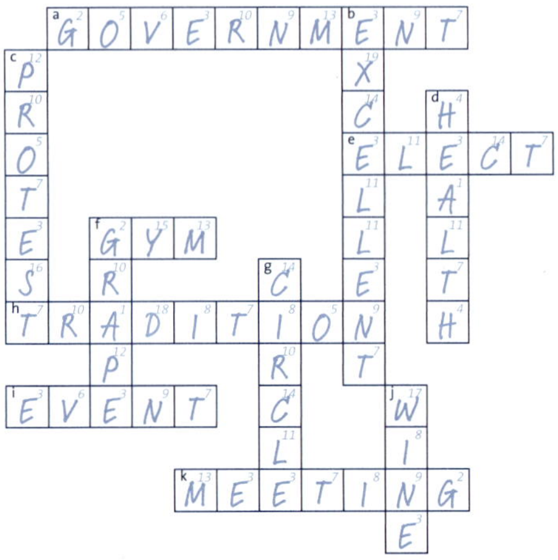

Wein – **j** down
Besprechung – **k** across
Regierung – **a** across
Turnhalle – **f** across
Ereignis – **i** across
Tradition – **h** across
privat – **g** down
ausgezeichnet – **b** down
Weintraube – **f** down
Gesundheit – **d** down
Fachschule – **e** across
Ernte – **c** down

17 Hour glasses

1		E	G	G	
2	G	U	I	D	E
3	F	A	R	T	H
4	S	I	L	L	Y
5		O	F	F	
			R		
6		L	I	E	
7	S	W	E	A	T
8	F	E	N	C	Y
9	T	O	D	A	Y
10		U	S	E	

1		I	C	E	
2	O	T	H	E	R
3	E	L	E	C	T
4	F	R	E	S	H
5		T	R	Y	
			L		
6		L	E	T	
7	G	R	A	D	E
8	V	I	D	E	O
9	E	V	E	N	T
10		C	R	Y	

Das geheime Wort lautet:
Englisch – cheerleader
Deutsch – Cheerleader

Unit 4

1 Word groups: Sports

people
champion, cheerleader, coach, footballer, goalkeeper, runner, supporter
places
court, ice rink, pitch, pool, running track, ski slope, stadium
activities
canoeing, climbing, hiking, hunting, riding, skating, skiing

2 Word ladder

surf – sure – sore – some – same – game – gate – late – lane – line – wine – wife – life – lift – list – fist – fast –last – lost – lose – rose – role – hole – **home**

3 Spot the mistakes

1 chanels: channels, cabel: cable
2 crimi: crime, serie: series
3 repeet: repeat, comedie: comedy
4 dokumentary: documentary, Afrikan: African
5 poeple: people, major: mayor
6 durring: during, zivil: civil
7 kandidates: candidates, their: there

4 Word pairs

break – plates
change – opinion
crash – car
debate – problems
found – college
get involved in – charity work
get to know – people
give up – smoking
offer – help
sign – letter
study – French
swap – stamps
tie – shoes
vote for – candidate

5 The best word

1 unbelievable, *2* guilty, *3* depressed, *4* polite, *5* active, *6* local, *7* broken, *8* foreign

6 More about...the Atlanta Olympics

1 be, *2* special, *3* anniversary, *4* for, *5* dollars, *6* built, *7* were, *8* crowd, *9* from, *10* over

7 Opposites

1 risen, *2* separate, *3* death, *4* unbelievable, *5* impolite, *6* violent, *7* soft, *8* minus, *9* dangerous, *10* illegal

8 Last letter – first letter

1 impressed, *2* drama, *3* archive, *4* explosion, *5* near, *6* research, *7* hurt, *8* terrorist, *9* throw, *10* war, *11* rise, *12* ending, *13* government

9 Crossword

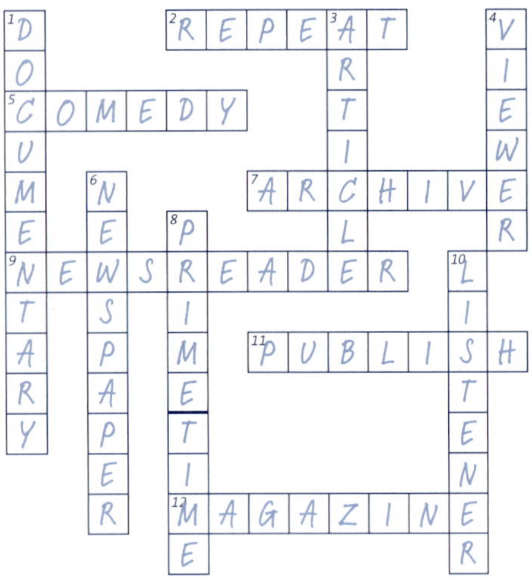

10 Synonyms

1 below/under, *2* clever/smart *3* dangerous/unsafe, *4* ill/sick, *5* gym/sports hall, *6* amazing/unbelievable *7* and so on/etc.

11 Odd word out

1 mayor, *2* network, *3* cotton, *4* dirty, *5* anniversary, *6* explosion, *7* during, *8* newsreader, *9* queue, *10* competition, *11* terrorist, *12* search engine, *13* exact, *14* traffic jam

12 Word search

I	M	S	R	C	E	X	B	N	K	W	V	T	S
P	A	R	L	I	A	M	E	N	T	E	O	D	M
D	Y	D	H	V	S	A	R	U	J	G	T	X	I
S	O	L	D	I	E	R	T	J	Q	U	E	E	N
F	R	B	M	L	P	C	L	N	K	D	E	R	O
C	V	P	M	R	Q	H	H	D	K	B	P	T	R
G	N	F	J	I	C	Y	U	I	I	X	R	X	I
O	B	R	I	G	O	V	E	R	N	M	E	N	T
V	M	E	S	H	K	X	H	X	G	V	S	N	Y
E	L	E	C	T	I	O	N	W	X	I	I	J	P
R	A	D	L	S	A	H	R	F	C	A	D	N	G
N	E	O	D	F	Y	C	P	R	O	T	E	S	T
O	B	M	R	H	N	L	P	J	U	U	N	Q	X
R	R	W	H	O	M	A	J	O	R	I	T	Y	T
S	F	C	K	E	T	W	C	N	T	T	B	G	R

parliament – Parlament
soldier – Soldat, **queen** – Königin
government – Regierung
election – Wahl
protest – Protest
majority – Mehrheit
governor – Gouverneur/in
mayor – Bürgermeister/in
freedom – Freiheit
civil rights – Bürgerrechte
march – Marsch, Demonstration
law – Gesetz
king – König
court – Gericht
vote – für jmd. Stimmen
president – Präsident/in
minority – Minderheit

13 Hour glasses

1		L	A	W	
2	S	I	N	C	E
3	L	O	C	A	L
4	O	T	H	E	R
5		F	O	R	
			R		
6		O	W	N	
7	C	R	O	W	D
8	C	O	M	I	C
9	A	P	A	R	T
10		E	N	D	

1		S	I	R	
2	C	A	M	E	L
3	H	U	M	A	N
4	P	R	E	S	S
5		A	D	D	
			I		
6		W	A	R	
7	M	O	T	E	L
8	B	R	E	A	K
9	S	A	L	A	D
10		G	Y	M	

Das geheime Wort lautet:
Englisch – immediately,
Deutsch – sofort

Hello and welcome! Ich bin der Wordmaster.
Hey! Wir helfen dir beim Wörter lernen.
Nachdem du neue Wörter in der Schule besprochen hast, kannst du die **New words** in diesem Buch als Vokabelheft benutzen.
Es gibt auch lustige Übungen. Die Lösungen findest du im beigelegten Heftchen.
Das große R bedeutet Revision: auf Deutsch Wiederholung. Hier übst du Vokabeln, die du bereits früher gelernt hast.
Tipps für die New words
1 Schau dir die Lücken im englischen Satz an. Welche neuen Wörter könnten passen?
2 Schau dir dann den deutschen Satz an. Die **fett gedruckten** Wörter zeigen, auf welches Wort es ankommt.
3 Wenn du mal nicht weiter weißt, kannst du auch im Vocabulary deines Schülerbuchs nachschlagen. Die Reihenfolge der Wörter dort hat dieselbe Reihenfolge wie die **New words**.
4 Im Vocabulary kannst du auch deine Lösungen überprüfen.
Introduction
New words ▸ p. 6–8
_______ ! We won our match!
A ______ is a kind of long valley.
The lake is very ______ – over 80 metres.
This street is 3.5 km long and 53 metres
The first flight across the Atlantic

Introduction

New words ▸ pp. 6 – 8

______________ ! We won our match!	**Stell dir vor!** Wir haben unser Spiel gewonnen!
A __________ is a kind of long valley.	Eine **Schlucht** ist eine Art langes Tal.
The lake is very __________ – over 80 metres.	Der See ist sehr **tief** – über 80 Meter.
This street is 3.5 km long and 53 metres _____ .	Diese Straße ist 3,5 km lang und 53 Meter **breit**.
The first flight across the Atlantic was ___ 1919.	Der erste Flug über den Atlantik war **im Jahre** 1919.
The show was __________ – everyone cheered.	Die Show war **klasse** – alle klatschten Beifall.
He's from Bonn – it's his __________________ .	Er kommt aus Bonn – das ist seine **Heimatstadt**.
I always ____________________ our holidays.	Ich **freue mich** immer **auf** unseren Urlaub.
The *Times* is a famous ________ newspaper.	Die *Times* ist eine berühmte **Tages**zeitung.
What __________ do I need to go camping?	Welche **Ausrüstung** brauche ich zum Zelten?
__________ the checkpoint at the gate	den Kontrollpunkt am Tor **passieren**
We need bus tickets for __________ 1 and 2.	Wir brauchen Busfahrkarten für **Zonen** 1 und 2.
stay for ____________________ to three weeks	**zweieinhalb** bis drei Wochen bleiben
He looked at me over the _______ of his glasses.	Er schaute mich über den **Rand** seiner Brille an.
You can go riding or _______ in the mountains.	Man kann reiten oder in den Bergen **wandern**.
take part in a 15-kilometre _______________	an einer 15-Kilometer **Wanderung** teilnehmen
Please mail us your __________ or suggestions.	Bitte mailt uns eure **Kommentare** oder Vorschläge.
_______________________ . How was your trip?	**Schön, dass du wieder da bist.** Wie war die Reise?

1 Spot the mistakes

In jedem Satz sind zwei Fehler. Unterstreiche und korrigiere sie.

1 Our swiming pool is 10 metres weid.	swimming	________
2 Gess what! I won a price for my English essay.	________	________
3 Do you no how diep this lake is?	________	________
4 Don't forgett to pack your sports geare.	________	________
5 The conzert was great – we had a really awsome time.	________	________

New words ▸ p. 9

Students in __________ 8 are about 14 years old.	Schüler in **Klasse 8** sind ungefähr 14 Jahre alt.
____________ money for a charity	Geld für eine Wohlfahrtsorganisation **sammeln**
Dad ____________ in the garden every week.	Im Garten **mäht** Papa jede Woche **den Rasen**.
Sheep and cows eat lots of __________ .	Schafe und Kühe fressen viel **Gras**.
You can buy lots of things cheaply at a ________ .	Im **Schlussverkauf** kann man vieles billig kaufen.
There was no hotel, so we slept in __________ .	Es gab kein Hotel, daher schliefen wir in **Zelten**.
Do you know _________________ this door?	Weißt du, **wie man diese Tür öffnet**?
He needs __________ to repair the clock.	Er braucht **Werkzeuge**, um die Uhr zu reparieren.
Many ____________________ live in Alaska.	Viele **amerikanische Ureinwohner** leben in Alaska.
There's a nice Beethoven ____________ in Bonn.	In Bonn gibt es ein schönes Beethoven**denkmal**.
I like _______ hair colours, not blue or purple.	Ich mag **natürliche** Haarfarben, nicht blau oder lila.
Everyone makes mistakes – it's only __________ .	Jeder macht Fehler – es ist nur **menschlich**.

2 More about ... The Grand Canyon Skywalk

Vervollständige den Text mit den Wörtern aus der Box.

build, expensive, kind, pay, steel, take, through, visitors

The Skywalk is a __________ (1) of bridge that sticks out about 20 metres over the rim of a side canyon at the Grand Canyon. It is *made of glass and __________ (2) and it looks like a big *horseshoe. There's a great view into the Grand Canyon and you can also look __________ (3) the glass floor to the ground over 1,000 metres below. But you mustn't __________ (4) photographs and you have to wear special shoes to protect the floor.

The Skywalk belongs to the Hualapai Indians. It opened for ____________ (5) in March 2007. Tickets cost about $25, but you also have to ____________ (6) over $50 for a one-mile bus trip, although this *includes lunch. Although the Skywalk is quite ____________ (7), a lot of tourists go there. The Hualapai are planning to ____________ (8) a museum, shops and hotels at the same place.

made of = hergestellt aus; horseshoe = Hufeisen; includes = schließt ... ein

3 Words in pictures: outdoor activities

Wie heißen die Gegenstände? Bei welcher Aktivität kann man sie benutzen?

1 boots – hiking ______

2 ______

3 ______

4 ______

5 ______

6 ______

7 ______

8 ______

9 ______

10 ______

4 Lost words

Ergänze die Sätze mit den Wörtern rechts.

1 We stayed __in__ a little village in the mountains.

2 One day we went ______ a long hike.

3 We walked ______ a mountain path for hours.

4 As we walked, we sang songs ______ German and English.

5 I was hungry, so I was looking forward ______ lunch.

6 We stopped ______ a picnic area ______ about 12.30 pm.

7 I had lots of sandwiches ______ my rucksack.

8 While we were eating we looked ______ our map.

9 We wanted to find the way back ______ the village.

10 In the end we got back ______ any problems.

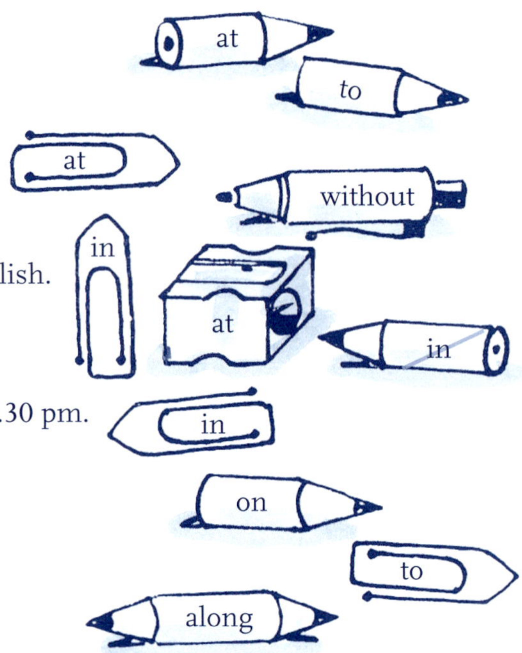

New words ▸ pp. 10–11

on the busy ______________ to New York	auf der **verkehrsreiche** Fernstraße nach New York
the fastest __________ from Cologne to Berlin	die schnellste **Strecke** von Köln nach Berlin
No car moves without ____________ .	Ohne **Benzin** fährt kein Auto.
You also get oil and air at ______________ .	An **Tankstellen** bekommt man auch Öl und Luft.
I'd like to buy a ________ of my holiday in Paris.	Ich möchte ein **Souvenir** vom Urlaub in Paris kaufen.
______________ are a kind of ID for cars.	**Nummernschilder** sind eine Art Ausweis für Autos.
Detroit is a centre of the US ________ industry.	Detroit ist ein Zentrum der US-**Auto**industrie.
There's a ___________ view from here.	Von hier hat man einen **eindrucksvollen** Ausblick.
She's very rich – she's a ________-millionaire.	Sie ist sehr reich – sie ist **Multi**millionärin.
He's six ________ tall – that's about 1 metre 83.	Er ist sechs **Fuß** groß – das sind etwa 1 Meter 83.
Birds have two _____________ .	Vögel haben zwei **Flügel**.
a beach at the northern ________ of the island	ein Strand an der nördlichen **Spitze** der Insel
Please ________ me. I didn't want to hurt you.	Bitte **vergib** mir! Ich wollte dich nicht verletzen.
an ____________ story like *Robinson Crusoe*	eine **Abenteuer**geschichte wie *Robinson Crusoe*

5 The best word

Finde in jeder Schublade das Wort, das am besten in die Lücke passt.

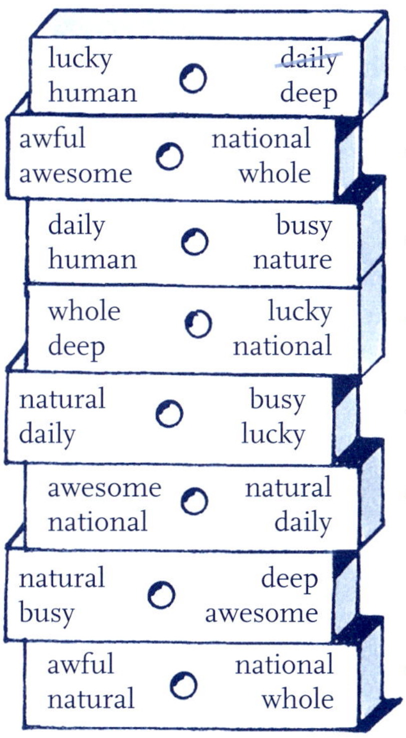

1 I read about the daily life of the Indians who had lived in the canyon.

2 I loved the view from the skywalk – it was really ____________ !

3 It's a ____________ road, especially at rush hour.

4 We stayed in Arizona for a ______________ week.

5 We were really ____________ – the weather was fantastic every day.

6 July 4th is the US ____________ holiday.

7 The water here is very ____________ so be careful if you can't swim.

8 I don't like artificial Christmas trees – ____________ ones are better.

6 German-English crossword

Across
- *2* abholen (4, 2)
- *6* Geld sammeln (5, 5)
- *7* wandern (4)
- *8* anhalten (4)
- *10* Rasen mähen (3, 3, 5)
- *12* ankommen, eintreffen (6)
- *13* zweieinhalb (3, 3, 1, 4)
- *14* Heimatstadt (8)

Down
- *1* vergeben, verzeihen (7)
- *2* schützen (4)
- *3* Ausrüstung (4)
- *4* sich auf (etwas) freuen (4, 6, 2)
- *5* raten, schätzen (5)
- *9* zeigen (4)
- *10* überqueren (5)
- *11* benutzen, verwenden (3)

7 Last letter – first letter

Der letzte Buchstabe von jedem Wort ist gleichzeitig der erste des nächsten Wortes.

- *1* Kommentar
- *2* Zelt
- *3* Werkzeug
- *4* Zuhörer
- *5* Kante, Rand
- *6* Denkmal
- *7* unterrichten
- *8* wandern
- *9* genug
- *10* menschlich
- *11* natürlich

8 Odd word out

Ein Wort passt nicht. Finde und unterstreiche es.

1 road – grade – route – street

2 toes – feet – centimetres – miles

3 canoe – comment – hike – cycle

4 awful – awesome – fantastic – grand

5 B&B – bed – hotel – motel

6 field – valley – human – mountain

7 tent – caravan – holiday flat – wing

8 deep – foggy – stormy – windy

9 forgive – run – swim – walk

10 clean – daily – neat – tidy

9 Word search

18 englische Begriffe aus den Wortfeldern „Natur“ und „Freizeit“ sind im Rätsel versteckt. Finde sie und übersetze sie ins Deutsche.

mountain – Berg

K	W	U	C	G	K	A	E	A	A	F	U	P
U	O	S	A	E	R	K	Q	S	W	I	M	J
M	O	U	N	T	A	I	N	B	F	E	X	L
C	D	E	O	Y	P	T	G	V	M	L	W	H
O	S	X	E	O	I	S	L	A	N	D	V	F
U	P	C	E	U	D	O	K	L	D	X	D	X
N	F	O	R	E	S	T	M	L	L	J	L	S
T	N	A	O	S	D	P	B	E	A	C	H	G
R	M	S	D	N	H	G	R	Y	Q	J	I	A
Y	M	T	R	T	I	U	Q	T	L	N	K	M
S	T	M	I	V	L	F	M	H	U	S	E	A
I	K	O	V	U	L	W	Y	C	B	K	X	J
D	I	K	E	V	V	G	L	O	L	I	M	X
E	Q	H	R	O	C	K	B	B	T	X	P	S

Unit 1

New words ▸ pp. 12–14

a wide ____________ with shops and cafés	eine breite **Allee** mit Läden und Cafés
We can buy a snack at the ____________ .	Wir können einen Snack im **Deli** kaufen.
The first ________ on the journey was at a café.	Der erste **Halt** auf der Reise war an einem Café.
Many ________________ hope for a new life.	Viele **Einwanderer** hoffen auf ein neues Leben.
I like to ________ in the sun on the beach.	Ich **liege** gerne am Strand in der Sonne.
Manhattan is New York's best known __________ .	Manhattan ist der bekannteste **Bezirk** New Yorks.
The ____________ will help you to find the house.	Die **Wegbeschreibung** hilft dir, das Haus zu finden.
I go shopping in big shops ____________ .	Ich kaufe in großen Läden **im Stadtzentrum** ein.
walk around the ____________ with the dog	mit dem Hund um den **Block** laufen
A ____________ is a path at the side of a road.	Ein **Bürgersteig** ist ein Weg neben einer Fahrbahn.
I stood in a long ____________ outside the cinema.	Ich stand in einer langen **Schlange** vor dem Kino.

1 Scrambled words: American and British English

Die Buchstabenrätsel ergeben Wörter aus dem amerikanischen Englisch. Trage diese und ihre britischen Entsprechungen ein. Die Tipps helfen dir.

		American English	British English	tip
1	edgar	grade	class	group of students
2	sag			'food' for cars
3	sag tatison			where you buy 'food' for cars
4	elin			You often see them at bus stops.
5	odontwnw			a city's heart
6	toua			not a bike
7	askwild			a path along the side of a road
8	aseemow			very, very good
9	nilcsee petal			letters and numbers on a car

2 Number crossword

Gleiche Zahlen sind gleiche Buchstaben.
Die angegebenen Lösungen helfen dir, das gesamte Rätsel zu lösen.

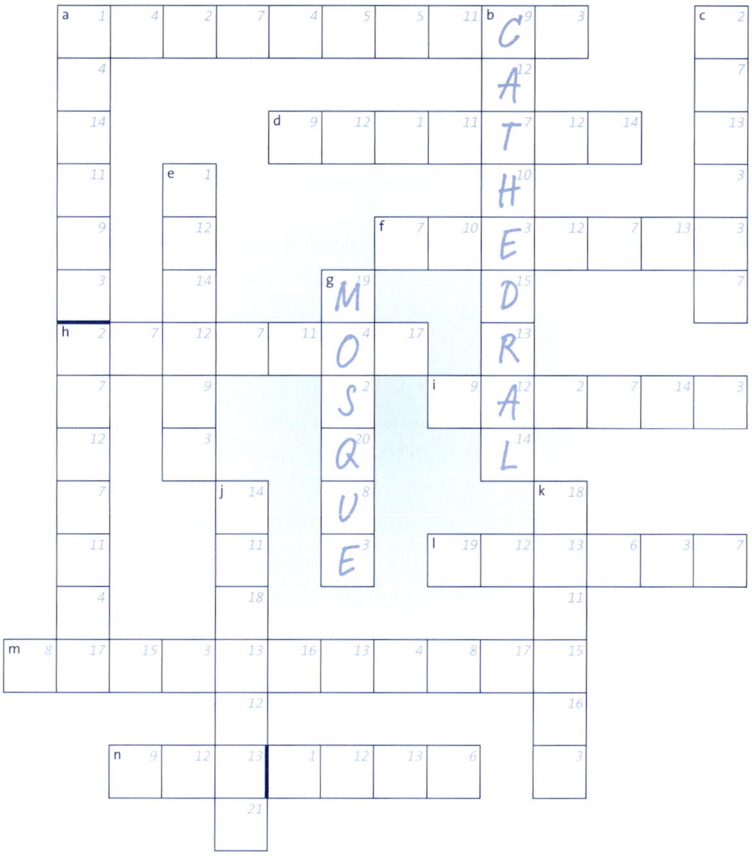

Wo im Rätsel findet man das englische Wort für

Brücke k down

Markt ______

Hauptstadt ______

Bahnhof ______

Postamt ______

Moschee ______

Palast ______

Schloss ______

Bibliothek ______

U-Bahn ______

Polizeiwache ______

Parkplatz ______

3 Verb forms

Ergänze die Tabelle der unregelmäßigen Verben.

1	lie	lay	lain	9	forget		
2		forgave		10		took	
3	catch			11	wear		
4			hidden	12			fed
5	meet			13	sing		
6		rode		14		drank	
7	put			15	tell		
8			felt	16			lost

New words ▸ p. 15

the ______ between town and country	der **Unterschied** zwischen Stadt und Land
70 firemen work at the ______ .	70 Feuerwehrmänner arbeiten an der **Feuerwache**.
Over 20 ______ hurried to the fire.	Über 20 **Feuerwehrleute** eilten zum Brand.
Jo wants to work ______ a fireman after school.	Jo will nach der Schule **als** Feuerwehrman arbeiten.
I hate milk. Is there ______ to drink?	Ich hasse Milch. Gibt's **etwas anderes** zu trinken?
Can you help me, please? – ______ , no problem!	Kannst du mir bitte helfen? – **Klar**, kein Problem!
You need water to ______ a fire.	Man braucht Wasser, um ein Feuer zu **löschen**.
work on the night ______ at a factory	Nacht**schicht** in einer Fabrik arbeiten
He's a nice ______ – everybody likes him.	Er ist ein netter **Kerl** – jeder mag ihn.
The ______ killed two men on the plane.	Der **Entführer** tötete zwei Männer im Flugzeug.
At 25 he ______ his father's company.	Mit 25 **übernahm** er die Firma seines Vaters.
The new ______ will be 612m high.	Der neue **Wolkenkratzer** wird 612m hoch sein.
Fires were ______ing all over the forest.	Im ganzen Wald **brannten** Feuer.
Our class trip will ______ next week.	Unser Klassenausflug **findet** nächste Woche **statt**.

4 Words in pictures

Zu jeder Lücke in den Sätzen passt ein Bild. Finde das Bild und trage das entsprechende Wort ein.

1 Firefighters wear helmets , not ______ .

2 Policemen catch ______ , not ______ .

3 Architects design ______ , not ______ .

4 Musicians play ______ , not ______ .

5 Photographers need ______ , not ______ .

5 What are the words?

Ergänze die Sätze mit den richtigen Wörtern.

1 Sorry, I can't help you. You'll have to ask somebody else.

2 OK, you went to the Empire State Building. And ________________ did you go?

3 This film's boring. Can't we watch ________________________ ?

4 I was the only guest at the party – ________________________ came.

5 We've bought fruit and vegetables. ________________ do we need?

6 We'll have to stay in this hotel – it's too expensive ________________________ .

7 Jake arrived late at the station, but ________________________ was there in time.

8 We've only got ten names on the list. ________________ can we invite?

6 Last letter – first letter

Der letzte Buchstabe von jedem Wort ist gleichzeitig der erste des nächsten Wortes.

1 Schlange, Reihe
2 beenden
3 Deli
4 Einwanderer
5 Spitze
6 Bürgersteig
7 tausend
8 Wegbeschreibung
9 Halt
10 arm
11 reich
12 Entführer
13 Strecke, Route

New words ▸ p. 16

See the cathedral in Cologne! ____________ !	Besucht den Dom in Köln! **Es ist ein Muss!**
Our flat is on the third ____________ .	Unsere Wohnung ist im dritten **Stock**.
A night at this hotel will ________ over £200.	Eine Nacht in diesem Hotel wird über £200 **kosten**.
Can I pay in US ____________ ?	Kann ich in US-**Dollar** bezahlen?
This skyscraper is the ____________ in the world.	Dieser Wolkenkratzer ist der **höchste** der Welt.
He's a ________ man, only about 1 metre 70.	Er ist **kleiner** Mann, nur etwa 1 Meter 70 groß.
Bank __________________ : 9 am to 6 pm	Bank**öffnungszeiten**: 9 Uhr bis 18 Uhr
____________ to museums is free on Sundays.	Der Museums**eintritt** ist sonntags kostenlos.
Hot and sunny! ________ weather for the beach.	Heiß und sonnig! **Ideales** Wetter für den Strand.
buy tickets at the __________________	Fahrkarten an der **Kasse** kaufen
Don't worry. ________________ .	Mach dir keine Sorgen. **Mir wird nichts passieren.**
Be quiet! I'm ____________ listening to you.	Sei still! Ich **habe es satt**, dir zuzuhören.

7 Hidden words

Ergänze die Wortgruppen, indem du Wörter mit Buchstaben der Wörter „fire station" bildest.

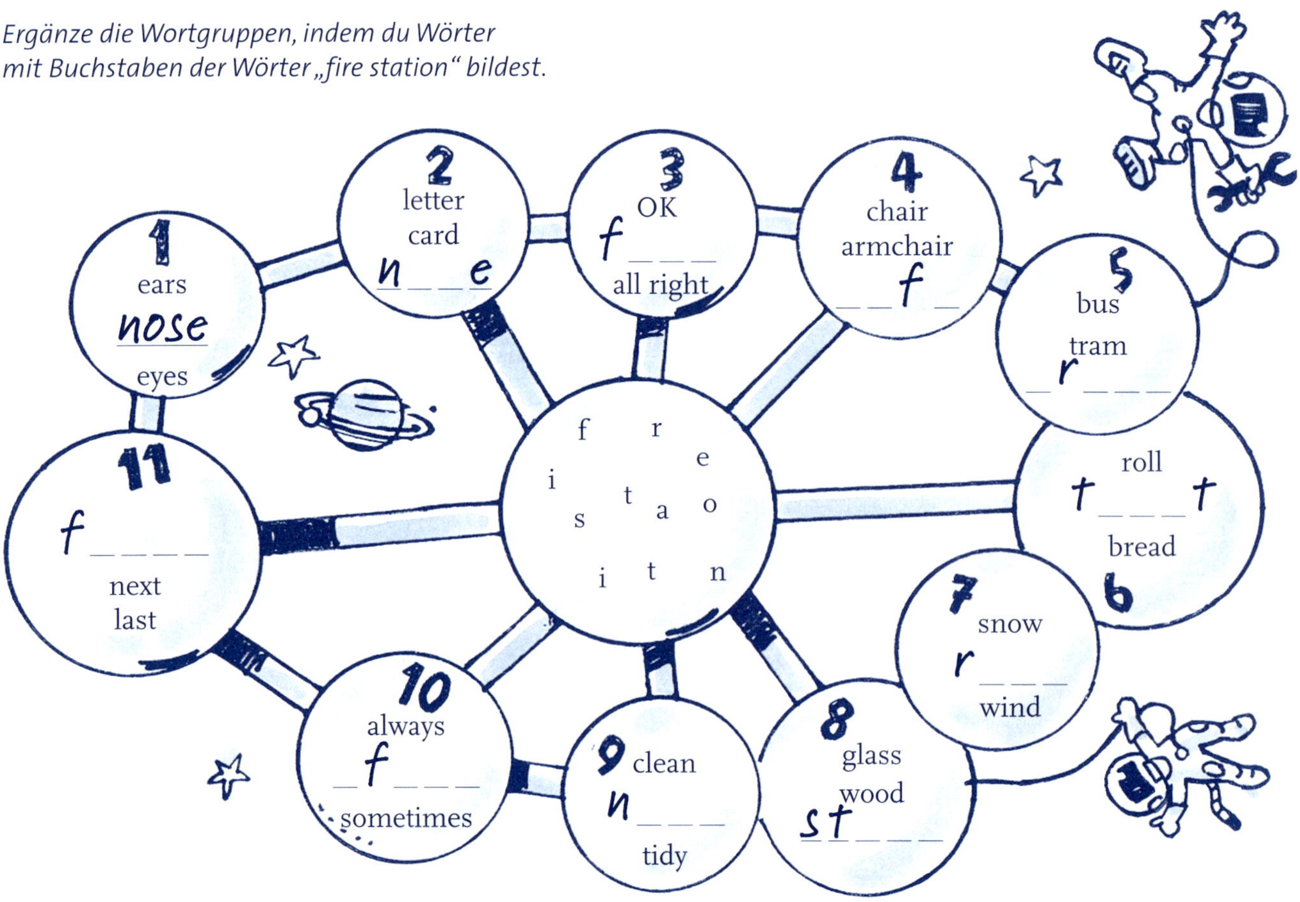

8 More about ... Remembering 9/11

Vervollständige den Text mit den Wörtern aus der Skyline.

near in touch who where whole work you

Every year on September 11, New York's skyline looks a little different. Between all the skyscrapers of Manhattan, ____________ (1) can see two huge columns of blue light – and these 'skyscrapers' really seem to reach the sky! On a cloudy day, they ____________ (2) the clouds and make them blue. The light comes from 88 very strong lamps ____________ (3) the place where the World Trade Centre stood before terrorists attacked it on September 11, 2001. This ____________ (4) of art is called 'Tribute in Light'. New Yorkers saw it for the first time ____________ (5) March 2002, when it lit up the night sky for a ____________ (6) month. Now the city turns it on just once a year, on September 11. Many New Yorkers like the two columns of light. They help them to *remember the people ____________ (7) died in the terrorist attacks. The 'Tribute in Light' costs $350,000 a year. Many people want to keep the tribute, but it is not clear ____________ (8) the money will come from.

remember sb. = jemandes gedenken

9 Hour glasses

Übersetze die Wörter und trage sie in die passende Sanduhr ein.

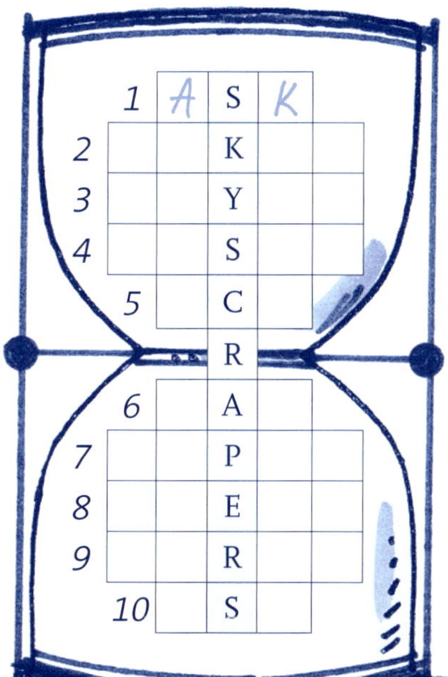

1 ausgeschaltet – bitten
2 täglich – Wanderungen
3 königlich – groß
4 gekränkt – putzen
5 Eis – ausgeschaltet
6 Alter – Stadtplan
7 andere(r, s) – Zeitung
8 Sahne – eintreten
9 Weide – März
10 Kunst – benutzen

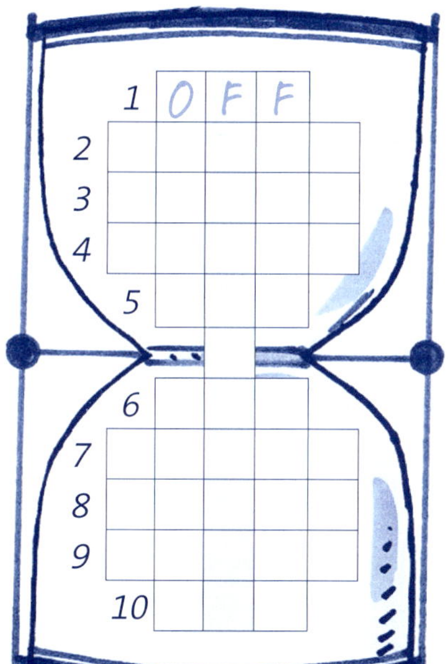

Das geheime Wort heißt: Englisch ____________________

Deutsch ____________________

New words ▸ p. 17

The beach is __________ with tourists in summer.	Der Strand ist **überfüllt** mit Touristen im Sommer.
__________ of people came to the stadium.	**Massen** von Menschen kamen ins Stadion.
Lots of New Yorkers eat __________ as a snack.	Viele New Yorker essen **Bagels** als Imbiss.
Bagels and __________ are very popular.	Bagels mit **Frischkäse** sind sehr beliebt.
Do you prefer milk or __________ ?	Nimmst du lieber Milch oder **Sahne**?
Would you prefer tea or __________ ?	Möchtest du lieber Tee oder **Kaffee**?
A shop assistant stood behind the __________ .	Eine Verkäuferin stand hinter der **Theke**.
There's a waiter! I'll __________ the drinks now.	Da ist ein Kellner! Ich **bestelle** jetzt die Getränke.
Which pizza do you want? Large or __________ ?	Welche Pizza willst du? Groß oder **normal**?
I'd like __________ , not normal water.	Ich möchte **Sprudel**, nicht normales Wasser.
The thief __________ the money and ran away.	Der Dieb **schnappte sich** das Geld und rannte weg.
Hanukkah is a __________ festival.	Chanukka ist ein **jüdisches** Fest.

10 Odd word out

Ein Wort passt nicht. Finde und unterstreiche es.

1 deli – pavement – juice bar – restaurant

2 downtown – road – street – avenue

3 large – big – short – huge

4 dollar – bank – euro – pound

5 B&B – bed – hotel – motel

6 sad – perfect – great – awesome

7 pavement – street – road – queue

8 harbour – fire station – train station – airport

9 firefighter – ranger – counter – hijacker

10 bagel – beef – lamb – pork

11 Spot the mistakes

In jedem Satz sind zwei Fehler. Unterstreiche und korrigiere sie.

1 It's better to sycle on the cycle path than on the pavment. cycle __________

2 There were twenty poeple in front of me in the queu. __________ __________

3 It was perfekt weather for a picknick in the mountains. __________ __________

4 We have a grand vew from our flat on the seventh flor. __________ __________

5 Do you need anything els? Or have you got evrything? __________ __________

12 Word search – Food and drink

Finde Begriffe aus dem Wortfeld „food and drink". (↓ →) Ordne sie der richtigen Gruppe zu und übersetze sie ins Deutsche.

B	I	S	C	U	I	T	X	S	S	Q	U	T	K	T
A	T	H	R	O	H	B	P	C	A	R	R	O	T	U
G	W	T	E	A	F	A	P	P	L	E	E	M	X	R
E	A	Q	A	J	J	V	O	G	M	E	H	A	Y	K
L	M	K	M	K	U	H	R	S	O	W	H	T	P	E
V	A	N	C	H	I	C	K	E	N	K	W	O	U	Y
G	T	P	H	J	C	I	G	L	H	J	A	O	Y	X
C	H	E	E	S	E	J	T	O	A	S	T	P	P	M
O	X	R	E	N	V	B	J	Q	T	M	E	N	W	U
F	C	A	S	T	R	A	W	B	E	R	R	Y	H	S
F	O	P	E	D	O	C	H	U	V	S	H	S	B	H
E	M	R	T	M	X	O	W	T	U	C	A	K	E	R
E	Q	O	N	I	O	N	W	T	U	O	A	Q	E	O
D	V	L	P	M	Y	O	V	E	P	L	B	S	F	O
H	L	L	A	M	B	J	B	R	E	A	D	A	O	M

Fruit and vegetables

carrot – Möhre

Drinks

tea – Tee

Milk products

cream cheese – Frischkäse

Meat and fish

chicken – Huhn

Bread, cake, etc.

bagel – Bagel

New words ▸ pp. 22–26

At 11 I ___________ short ___________ from work.	Um 11 **mache** ich **eine** kurze **Pause** von der Arbeit.
Where can small children play in ___________ ?	Wo können kleine Kinder in **Sicherheit** spielen?
Try to _____________ what the number means.	Versuche **herauszufinden**, was die Zahl bedeutet.
show a word in its _________________________	ein Wort in seinem **Zusammenhang** zeigen
There are lots of wild animals at London _______ .	Im Londoner **Zoo** gibt es viele wilde Tiere.
Millions of years ago _____________ lived here.	Vor Millionen Jahren lebten hier **Dinosaurier**.
a huge ______________________ of model planes	eine riesige **Sammlung** von Modellflugzeugen
Russia's the biggest country ________________ .	Russland ist das größte Land **der Welt**.
Some footballers ________ millions every year.	Einige Fußballspieler **verdienen** Millionen im Jahr.
He lives in a two-room _____________ in Boston.	Er wohnt in einer 2-Zimmer-**Wohnung** in Boston.
Why did you ________________ to move?	Warum habt ihr euch **entschieden**, umzuziehen?
He's yawning again – he ___________ to be tired.	Er gähnt wieder – er **scheint** müde zu sein.
He looks so ill – maybe he's ________________ .	Er sieht so krank aus – vielleicht **nimmt** er **Drogen**.
I've eaten something wrong – I _____________ .	Ich habe was Falsches gegessen – **mir ist schlecht**.

13 Words with different meanings

Finde in der Liste die passenden Wörter zu den Paaren 1–8.
Trage sie ein und unterstreiche die deutschen Entsprechungen.

1
a) in der dritten Zeile
b) eine Schlange vor dem Kino
line

2
a) eine Zeitzone überqueren
b) Bist du sauer auf mich?
____

3
a) Das ist ein sehr hohes Gebäude.
b) Mein Bruder ist fast 2 Meter groß.
____

4
a) die nördliche Spitze der Insel
b) ein guter Tipp für den Urlaub in New York
____

5
a) eine kurze Pause machen
b) Gläser kaputt machen
____

6
a) Kleider vom Boden aufheben
b) im 6. Stock wohnen
____

break
cross
floor
~~line~~
tall
tip

14 Pronunciation

Wie wird das /a/ ausgesprochen? Ordne die Wörter aus der Schnecke der richtigen Aussprachegruppe zu.

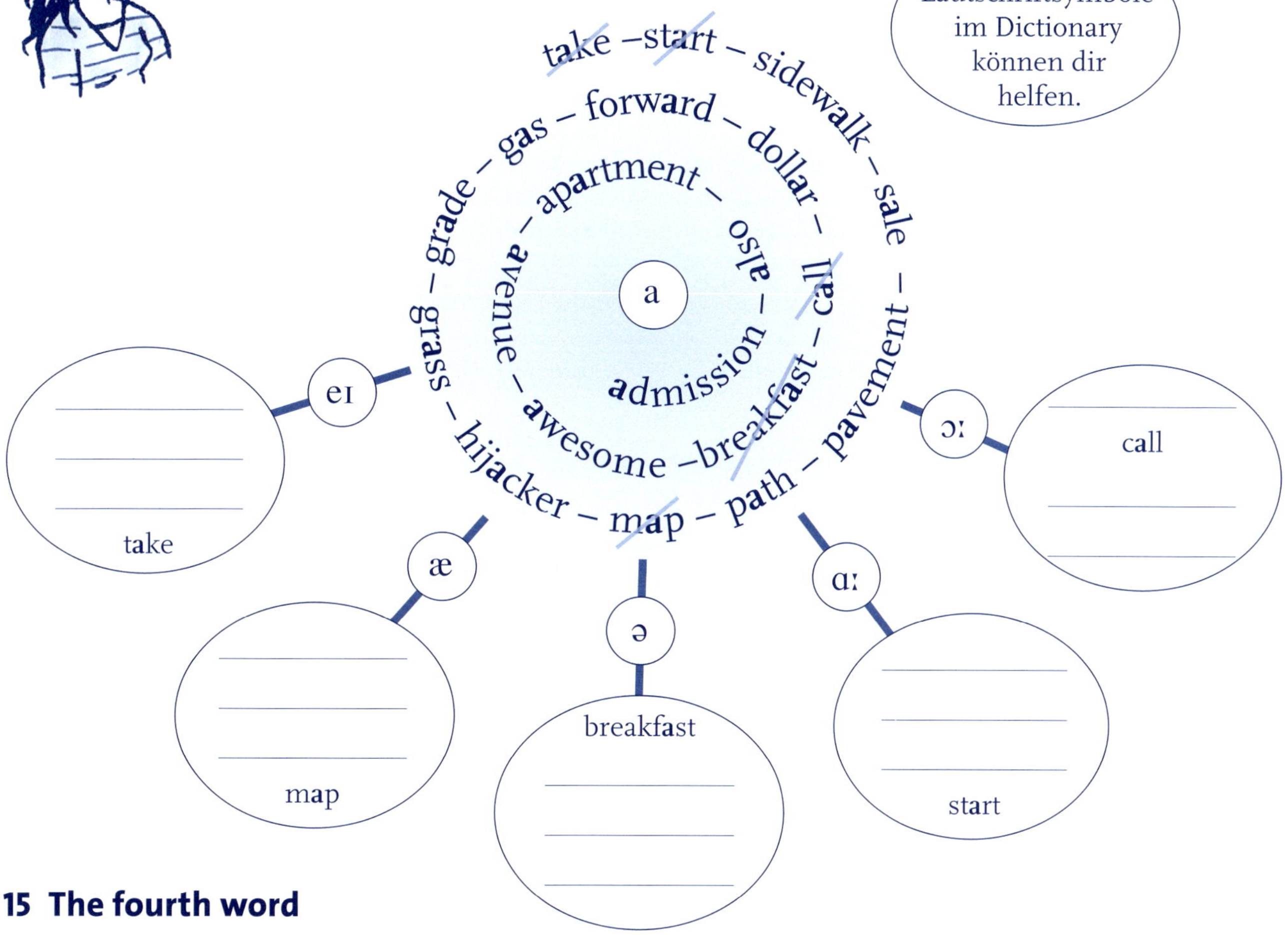

15 The fourth word

Welches Wort fehlt hier?

1 describe – description	collect –	collection	*9* 14–18 – high school	11–14 –	______
2 walk – feet	fly –	______	*10* wind – blow	fire –	______
3 finger – hand	toe –	______	*11* food – supermarket	petrol –	______
4 Germany – euro	US –	______	*12* food – supermarket	ticket –	______
5 Germany – kilometre	US –	______	*13* chicken – meat	salmon –	
6 small – large	short –	______	*14* lunch – meal	chicken curry –	______
7 GB – ground floor	US –	______	*15* hospital – doctor	firestation –	______
8 top – above	bottom –	______	*16* sing – song	sell –	______

New words ▸ p. 27

Give Dad a ________ and say good night!	Gib Papa einen **Kuss** und sag gute Nacht.
When will the princess ________ the frog?	Wann wird die Prinzessin den Frosch **küssen**?
A ________ ran down her cheek.	Eine **Träne** lief ihre Wange herunter.
He was very sad and started to ________ .	Er war sehr traurig und fing an zu **weinen**.
Did you ________ how she looked at you?	Hast du **bemerkt**, wie sie dich angeschaut hat?
The old man had a long white ________ .	Der alte Mann hatte einen langen weißen **Bart**.
Does everyone in Norway have ________ hair?	Haben alle in Norwegen **blonde** Haare?
He hit him, and ________ him with his boots.	Er schlug ihn und **trat** ihn mit seinen Stiefeln.
He took his ________ and shot the bear.	Er nahm sein **Gewehr** und erschoss den Bär.
His telephone number is ________ his address,	Seine Telefonnummer steht **unter** seiner Adresse,
... and his name is ________ his address.	... und sein Name ist **über** der Adresse.
Is that ________ or ketchup on your shirt?	Ist das **Blut** oder Ketchup an deinem Hemd?
I ________ a piece of bread and ate it quickly.	Ich **riss** ein Stück Brot **ab** und aß es schnell.
Your ________ are under your eyes.	Die **Wangen** findet man unter den Augen.
The last bus has left. Can I ________ ?	Der letzte Bus ist weg. Kann ich **ein Taxi nehmen**?

16 Word friends

In jedem Haus gibt es drei Wörter bzw. Wortverbindungen, die man direkt nach dem Verb auf der Fahne benutzen kann. Unterstreiche sie.

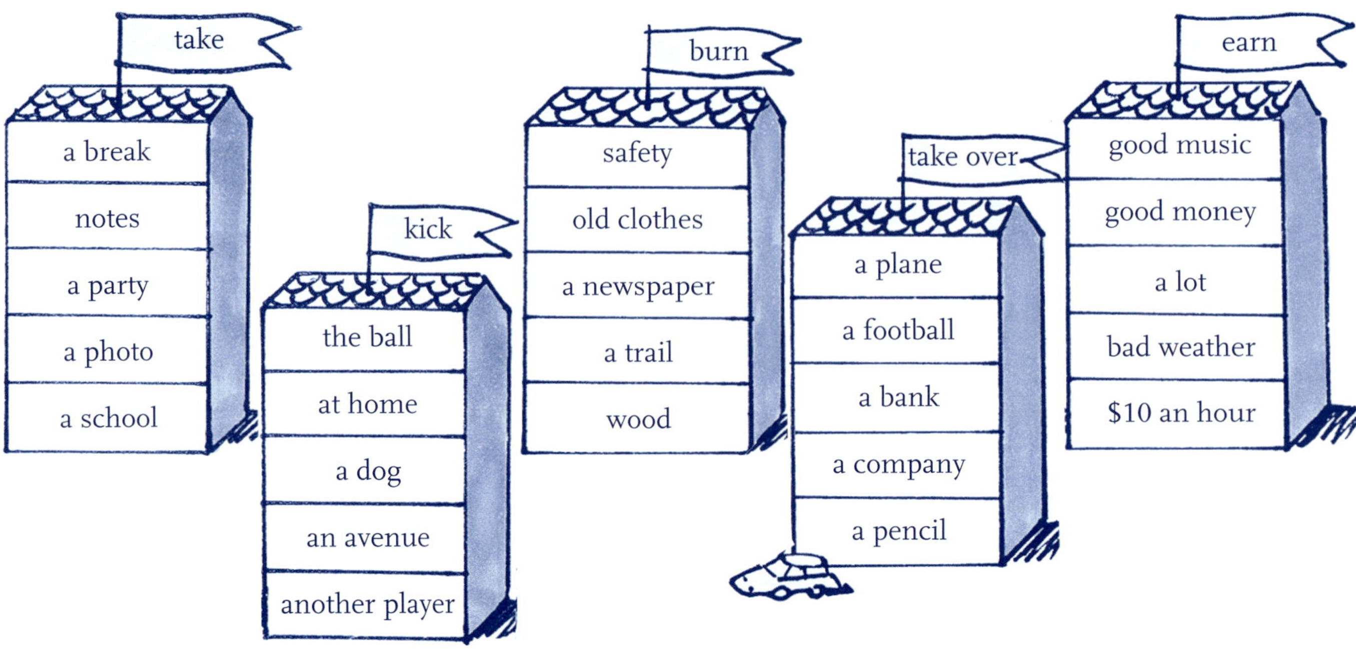

New words ▸ pp. 28–29

We can sit on a __________ in the park.	Wir können uns auf eine **Bank** im Park sezten.
a short holiday – just __________________ days	ein Kurzurlaub – nur **ein paar** Tage
A _____________ is more fun if everyone talks.	Ein **Gespräch** macht mehr Spaß, wenn alle reden.
The information isn't correct – it's ________ !	Die Angaben sind nicht richtig – sie sind **falsch**!
Please help me to _____________ my English.	Hilf mir bitte, mein Englisch zu **verbessern**.

17 Word ladder

Gehe von unten nach oben, indem du auf jeder Sprosse einen Buchstaben veränderst.

There's too much ★ on these chips.

I bought these jeans in the winter ★ .

The club meets on the ★ day every week.

We need ★ milk and butter from the shop.

Poor Jake's got a temperature and a ★ throat.

I think New York is ★ interesting than Washington.

We have a ★ in our garden – it makes little hills on the grass.

1 ★ = 1,609 metres

This pen isn't ★ – is it yours?

★ your own business!

Cycling against the ★ was difficult.

That poor bird can't fly – it's hurt its left ★ .

The ★ and queen have just arrived.

It was ★ of scary alone in the park at night.

Did you ★ the book you were looking for?

I was ill yesterday, but I'm ★ again today.

BE queue = AE ★

What kind of music do you ★ ?

We went on a long ★ in the mountains.

The bank robbers looked for a place to ★ the money.

We live on the sunny ★ of the street.

I'd like to be able to ★ a horse.

18 Lost words

Ergänze die Sätze mit den Wörtern auf den Bällen.

1 **Did** you know that Frank is scared _of_ mice?

2 **Are** you looking forward ________ your holiday?

3 **How** long did it take to put ________ the fire?

4 **Can** you help me to work ________ the answer to this question?

5 I heard a funny noise ________ the middle of the night.

6 **I'd** like to spend a couple ________ days in New York.

7 I was tired ________ waiting for the bus, so I decided to walk.

19 Word groups

Trage die Wörter aus der Wolke in die richtigen Sterne ein.

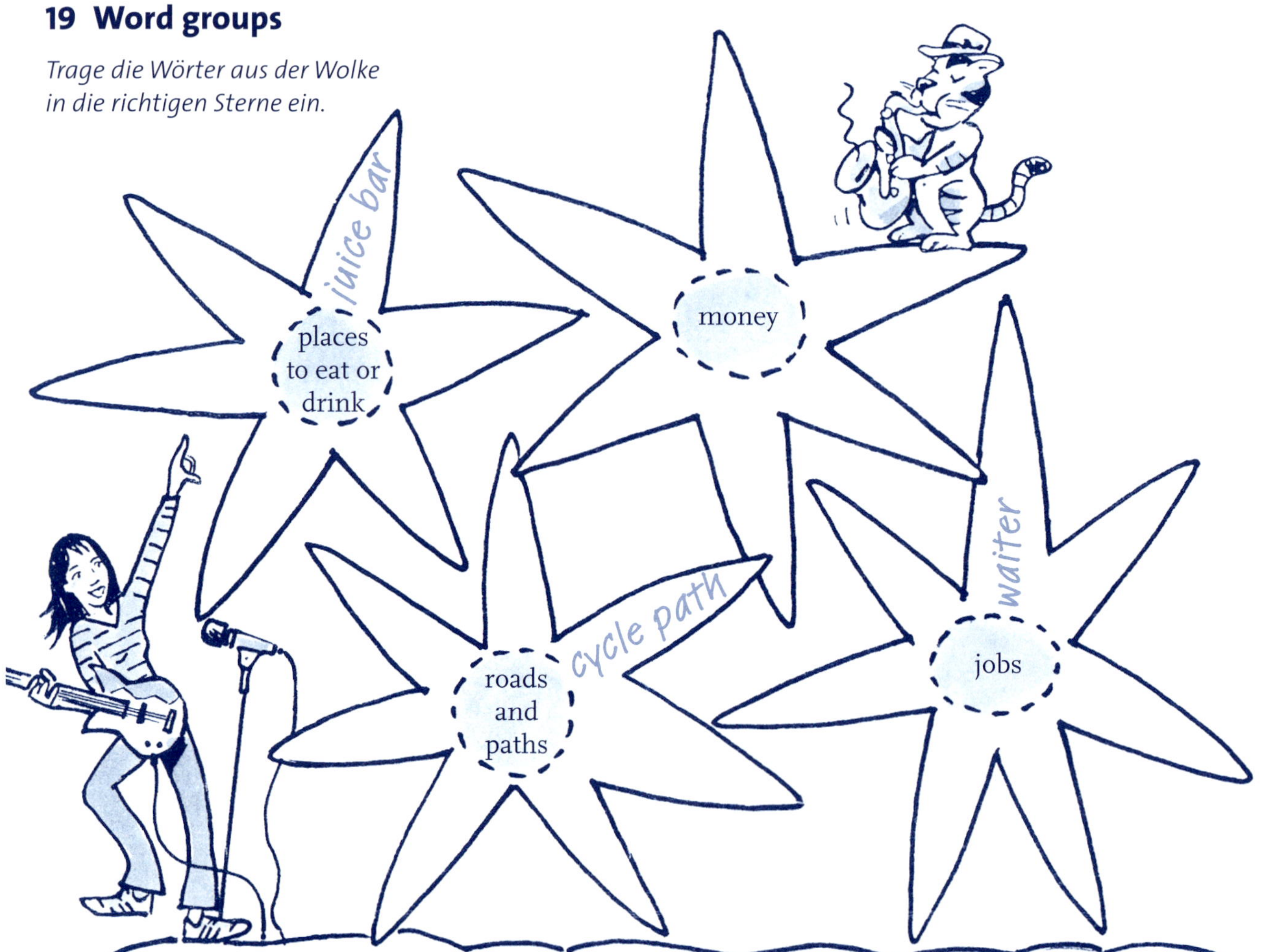

avenue café canteen cent ~~cycle path~~ deli dollar editor euro firefighter highway ~~juice bar~~ musician pavement policeman pence penny pound pub ranger road restaurant route street ~~waiter~~ waitress

New words ▸ pp. 34–35

I love the __________ leaves on trees in autumn.	Ich mag die **goldenen** Blätter an Bäumen im Herbst.
Long ago money was made of __________ .	Vor langer Zeit wurde Geld aus **Gold** gemacht.
The _______________ made thousands homeless.	Das **Erdbeben** machte Tausende obdachlos.
Our planet is called _____________ .	Unser Planet heißt **Erde**.
_______________ kids often sleep under bridges.	**Obdachlose** Kinder schlafen oft unter Brücken.
Each state in the US has a _______________ .	Jeder US-Bundesstaat hat einen **Gouverneur**.
We're just crossing the _____________ to Texas.	Gerade überqueren wir die **Grenze** nach Texas.

1 Words in pictures

Ordne die Verben in der Box dem richtigen Bild zu.

cry kiss explain scream shout whisper

1 ____________________

2 ____________________

3 ____________________

4 ____________________

5 ____________________

6 ____________________

2 Odd word out

Ein Wort passt nicht. Finde und unterstreiche es.

1 cat – <u>dinosaur</u> – hamster – rabbit

2 safety – salad – sandwich – sausage

3 dollar – earn – euro – pound

4 arm – blood – foot – leg

5 cry – cycle – run – walk

6 elephant – lion – tiger – zoo

7 a couple – a few – a lot – a pair

8 beard – blond – brown – dark

9 correct – false – OK – right

10 bench – chair – earth – sofa

3 Word search

Finde Begriffe aus dem Wortfeld „travel and tourism". (↓ →)
Ordne sie der richtigen Gruppe zu.

C	A	T	H	E	D	R	A	L	X	B	U	S	J	N	U	M
S	B	R	O	C	H	U	R	E	W	O	E	J	M	A	B	O
I	R	P	L	A	N	E	B	B	B	A	M	I	X	T	A	T
M	B	F	X	U	M	M	T	I	E	T	E	N	T	I	C	E
O	A	V	A	X	O	U	V	K	D	N	P	A	R	O	K	L
H	Y	N	Q	G	S	G	U	E	&	H	I	Y	A	N	P	K
O	S	J	Y	N	Q	W	C	A	B	I	N	V	I	A	A	R
L	S	J	H	D	U	F	C	A	R	A	V	A	N	L	C	U
I	U	H	O	T	E	L	Q	E	E	W	S	A	B	P	K	C
D	I	X	B	Y	C	H	C	L	A	Y	C	R	R	A	G	K
A	T	H	S	M	V	Q	A	R	K	C	A	D	J	R	L	S
Y	C	O	Q	U	X	F	S	M	F	E	R	R	Y	K	L	A
F	A	S	U	S	D	E	T	K	A	N	Q	Q	D	D	Y	C
L	S	T	C	E	I	H	L	G	S	H	I	P	U	F	I	K
A	E	E	N	U	T	E	E	A	T	I	C	K	E	T	S	X
T	U	L	O	M	O	N	U	M	E	N	T	M	M	M	A	P

places to see or visit

national park

things to take with you

map

ways to travel

plane

where to sleep

bed & breakfast

New words ▸ p. 36

How long has he worked in the car ____________ ?	Wie lange arbeitet er schon im Auto**handel**?
____________ is important in the country.	Die **Landwirtschaft** ist auf dem Lande wichtig.
Essen is a big German ________________ city.	Essen ist eine große deutsche **Industriestadt**.
Detroit is a centre of the US auto ____________ .	Detroit ist ein Zentrum der US-Auto**industrie**.
Would you prefer to drink red or white _______ ?	Würdest du lieber Rot- oder Weiß**wein** trinken?
I want to _______ a _______ at it before I buy it.	Ich will es **ansehen**, bevor ich es kaufe.
He sells ____________ like coffee and chocolate.	Er verkauft **Produkte** wie Kaffee und Schokolade.
Texas is known for the ________________ of oil.	Texas ist für die **Produktion** von Öl bekannt.
The Eiffel Tower is a big _________ in Paris.	Der Eiffelturm ist eine große **Attraktion** in Paris.
____________ are grown along the Mosel.	Entlang der Mosel werden **Weintrauben** angebaut.

4 Definitions

Vervollständige die Definitionen mit Wörtern aus der linken Sprühwolke. Trage die Lösungen aus der anderen Sprühwolke in die rechte Spalte ein.

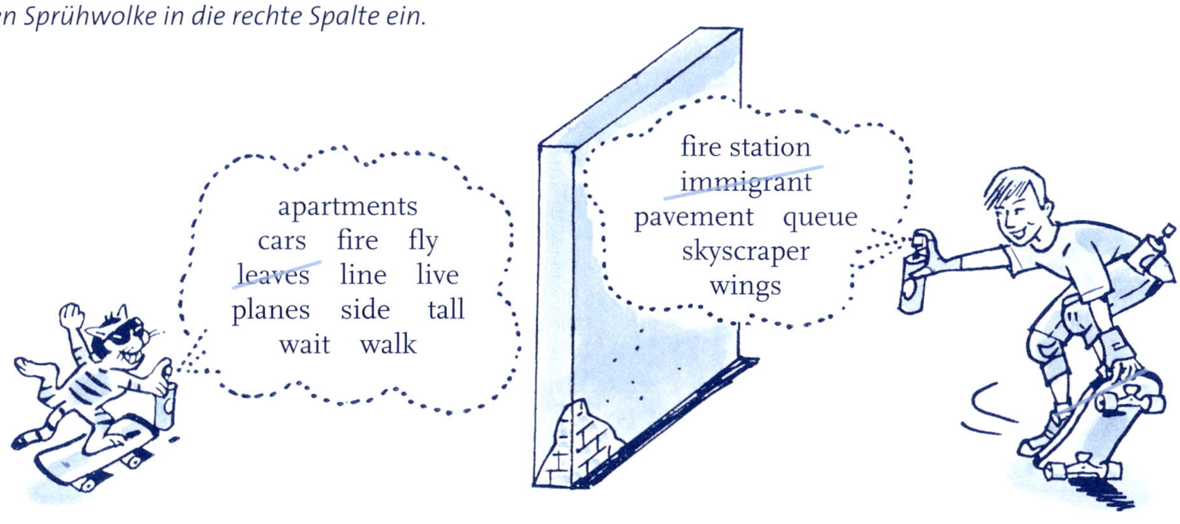

1 a person who leaves his own country and comes to ______ in your country immigrant

2 a very _________ building with lots of offices or _________ ____________

3 a _________ of people or _________ waiting for something ____________

4 a building where firefighters _________ until they have to put out a _______ ____________

5 a path at the _________ of a road where people can _________ safely ____________

6 something that birds and _________ need to _________ ____________

5 Scrambled words: On a farm

Die Buchstabenrätsel ergeben Verben, die landwirtschaftliche Arbeit beschreiben können. Benutze sie, um die Sätze zu vervollständigen.

1	U C T	Farmers cut long grass and use it as animal food.
2	P A R P R E E	You have to ________ the ground before you plant the vegetables.
3	P E K E	A lot of farmers in this area ________ cows and sheep.
4	E F E D	The pigs are hungry – it's time to ________ them.
5	O L O K F A T E R	We have sheepdogs to ________ the sheep.
6	P O D R C U E	These farmers ________ thousands of litres of milk every week.
7	R O W G	A lot of farmers in the Netherlands ________ tomatoes.
8	S E U	Can you ________ machines to pick apples?
9	L E L S	We ________ our milk to big supermarkets.
10	L I L K	We have to ________ insects because they attack our plants.
11	K A P C	Farm workers ________ the fruit in boxes before it goes to the market.
12	K E M A	If we have too many apples we use them to ________ juice.

6 Spot the mistakes

In jedem Satz sind zwei Fehler. Unterstreiche und korrigiere sie.

1 If your tired, we can take a brake for ten minutes. you're ________

2 Some people drink wein with there meals. ________ ________

3 The Brandenburg Gait is a big attraktion in Berlin. ________ ________

4 Would you like creme in your koffee? ________ ________

5 You can by our produkts online. ________ ________

New words ▸ *p. 37*

I learned a lot about American art and ________ .	Ich lernte viel über amerikanische Kunst und **Kultur**.
She has a positive ________ towards work.	Sie hat eine positive **Einstellung** zur Arbeit.
A small ________ in Belgium speaks German.	Eine kleine **Minderheit** in Belgien spricht Deutsch.
A ________ of kids prefer TV to radio.	Eine **Mehrheit** der Kinder zieht TV dem Radio vor.
He's different, but he's trying to ________ .	Er ist anders, aber er versucht, **sich anzupassen**.
Are you a ________ of this club?	Bist du **Mitglied** in diesem Club?
Other kids ________ him because he's so fat.	Andere Kinder **lachen** ihn **aus**, weil er so dick ist.
He has ten years' teaching ________ .	Er hat zehn Jahre Unterrichts**erfahrung**.
It's the worst storm I've ever ________ .	Es ist der schlimmste Sturm, den ich je **erlebt** habe.
This pen isn't mine. Does it ________ to you?	Dieser Füller ist nicht meiner. **Gehört** er dir?
Many ________ minorities live in London.	In London wohnen viele **ethnische** Minderheiten.
He was born in Bonn and is a German ________ .	Er ist in Bonn geboren und deutscher **Staatsbürger**.
discuss advantages and ________	Vor- und **Nachteile** diskutieren
Is it an ________ to have rich parents?	Ist es ein **Vorteil**, reiche Eltern zu haben?
Do you ________ well? – Yes, we're good mates.	**Versteht** ihr euch gut? – Ja, wir sind gute Kumpel.
End ________ against minorities!	Beendet **Diskriminierung** gegenüber Minderheiten!
The old laws ________ against women.	Die alten Gesetze **diskriminieren** Frauen.
Religious ________ is still a problem.	Religiöse **Vorurteile** sind immer noch ein Problem.
He's ________ against minorities.	Er ist **voreingenommen** gegenüber Minderheiten.
You have to work hard to ________ .	Du musst hart arbeiten, um **Erfolg** zu **haben**.
Try to ________ like an adult!	Versuche, dich wie ein Erwachsener zu **verhalten**!
a big city with a ________ of 7 million	eine große Stadt mit 7 Millionen **Einwohnern**

7 Word families

Finde die passenden Nomen zu den angegebenen Verben.

1 draw – drawing
2 produce – ______
3 kiss – ______
4 argue – ______
5 succeed – ______
6 attack – ______
7 spell – ______
8 hike – ______
9 revise – ______
10 collect – ______
11 translate – ______
12 discriminate – ______

8 Last letter – first letter

Der letzte Buchstabe von jedem Wort ist gleichzeitig der erste des nächsten Wortes.

1 schnappen
2 gehören
3 Weintraube
4 ethnisch
5 Wange
6 küssen
7 klein (Person)
8 groß (Person)
9 lachen
10 obdachlos
11 Sicherheit
12 Hof
13 Nachteil

9 Opposites

Trage das Gegenteil der fett gedruckten Wörter in die Lücken ein.

1 **blond** / dark hair
2 a **dangerous** / ______ place for swimmers
3 a **tall** / ______ man
4 a big **majority**/ a small ______
5 a great **advantage**/ ______
6 **start** / ______ a fire
7 **above** / ______ the line
8 the **least** / ______ interesting thing
9 **bad at** / ______ at swimming
10 **win** / ______ a difficult game

New words ▸ p. 38

A ____________ cuts the grass twice a month.	Ein **Gärtner** mähnt den Rasen zweimal im Monat.
He had big problems and had to _____ for help.	Er hatte große Probleme und musste um Hilfe **bitten**.
The ____________ wants to build more schools.	Die **Regierung** will mehr Schulen bauen.
We built a ____________ around our garden.	Wir bauten einen **Zaun** um unseren Garten.
Many Mexicans enter the USA ____________ly .	Viele Mexikaner reisen **illegal** in die USA ein.
Is it __________ to copy your own CDs?	Ist es **legal**, eigene CDs zu kopieren?
Let's share the cake – I'll give you _________ it.	Lass uns den Kuchen teilen. Ich gebe dir **die Hälfte**.
It's boring here because there's so _______ to do.	Es ist langweilig hier, weil es so **wenig** zu tun gibt.
Illegal immigrants are hoping for an _________ .	Illegale Immigranten hoffen auf eine **Amnestie**.

10 More about ... Los Angeles

Vervollständige den Text mit den Wörtern aus der Box.

In 1781, 44 Spanish-speaking *settlers *founded the city of *El Pueblo de Nuestra Senora la Reina de Los Angeles del Rio de la Porciuncula*. Today we __________ (1) this city just as Los Angeles or L.A. The population is now about 4 million, and another 13 million people __________ (2) in the Los Angeles *metropolitan area.

L.A. is California's largest city and the second __________ (3) city in the US. The metropolitan area is over 12,000 square kilometres, almost half the ____________ (4) of Belgium. People from all over the world live in L.A. The two ______________ (5) languages are English and Spanish, but over 200 ____________ (6) languages are also spoken. L.A. is one of the world's most important *economic centres. And of course Hollywood, in the north of the metropolitan area, is the world ____________ (7) of the film industry. Hundreds of TV shows and video games are also made in the city, and music plays a big role __________ (8).

settler = Siedler; found = gründen; metropolitan area = Ballungsraum; economic centre = Wirtschaftszentrum

New words ▸ p. 42–48

Awesome is a __________ for great.	*Awesome* ist ein **Synonym** für *great*.
The summer ______ has lots of outdoor activities.	Das Sommer**lager** bietet viele Aktivitäten im Freien.
Excuse me. I'm looking for a __________ book.	Entschuldigen Sie. Ich suche ein **bestimmtes** Buch.
If you're a __________ , you never eat meat.	Wenn man **Vegetarier** ist, isst man nie Fleisch.
The new '__________ of the Year' is a swimmer.	Der neue „**Sportler** des Jahres" ist ein Schwimmer.
You mustn't do that – it's against the __________ .	Das darfst du nicht – es ist gegen die **Vorschriften**.
Dear ______ or ________ , ...	Sehr geehrte **Damen** und **Herren**, ...
... Yours __________	... **Mit freundlichen Grüßen**
Dear Mrs Cox, ... Yours __________	Sehr geehrte Frau Cox, ... **Mit freundlichen Grüßen**
When did Columbus __________ America?	Wann hat Columbus Amerika **entdeckt**?
He __________ into another car.	Er ist mit einem Auto **zusammengestoßen**.
He was __________ about the bad news.	Er war über die schlechte Nachricht **schockiert**.
Steven Spielberg is a famous __________ .	Steven Spielberg ist ein berühmter **Regisseur**.
There's no danger, so __________ !	Es gibt keine Gefahr, also **bleib ruhig**.

11 Synonyms

Finde für jede Lücke zwei Synonyme. Trage sie ein.

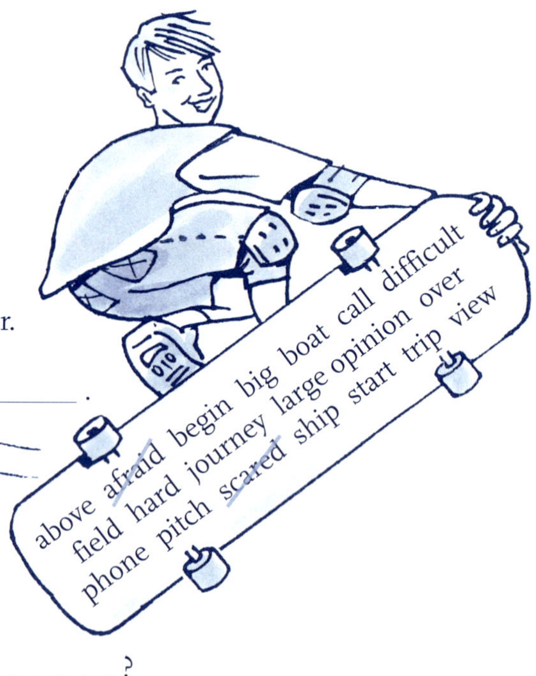

1. Are you really afraid / scared of mice?
2. Our flat isn't __________ / __________ enough for all of us.
3. I'll __________ / __________ him if you give me his number.
4. The theme park is a bit expensive in my __________ / __________ .
5. This exercise is quite __________ / __________ .
6. The film doesn't __________ / __________ until 10 pm.
7. How was your __________ / __________ to Los Angeles?
8. Is it cheaper to fly to England than to go by __________ / __________ ?
9. There are only 21 players on the __________ / __________ right now.
10. The Browns live in a flat __________ / __________ their shop.

New words ▸ p. 49

The Pacific __________ is west of America.	Der Pazifische **Ozean** ist westlich von Amerika.
The west coast of France is on the __________ .	Die Westküste Frankreichs liegt am **Atlantik**.
I expected him at four, but he didn't __________ .	Ich erwartete ihn um vier, aber er **erschien** nicht.
How can you keep yourself warm in the _____ ?	Wie hält man sich in der **Kälte** warm?
The bed is very ____________ , so I sleep well.	Das Bett ist sehr **bequem**, also schlafe ich gut.
This chair is so _______ – nobody sits there.	Der Stuhl ist so **unbequem** – keiner setzt sich dahin.
The car won't start – the __________ is broken.	Das Auto startet nicht – der **Motor** ist kaputt.
Please _________________ that the light is out.	**Vergewissere dich** bitte, dass das Licht aus ist.
You can do anything – ____________ you like!	Du darfst alles machen – **was auch immer** du magst.
We work every day ____________ Sunday.	Wir arbeiten jeden Tag **außer** Sonntag.

12 Word ladder

Gehe von unten nach oben, indem du bei jeder Sprosse einen Buchstaben veränderst.

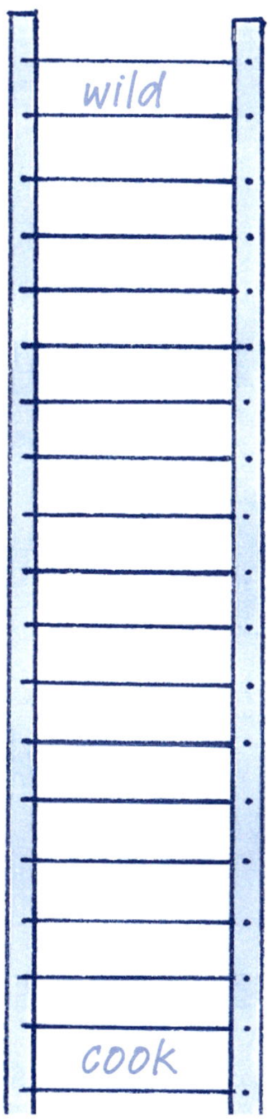

You can see lots of ★ animals in the forest.
It's difficult to cycle against a strong ★.
You can buy Californian ★ in Germany.
British English: queue / American English: ★
I'd be afraid to walk down that dark ★ at night.
There was so much fog that the plane couldn't ★ .
Which instrument does your sister play in the ★ ?
Mum has just gone to the ★ to get some money.
He left by the ★ door so that nobody would see him.
I still have to ★ my suitcase.
I can ★ you up at the station, if you like.
Stop! You mustn't ★ the dog!
I was too ★ to go to school yesterday.
I can see your toe through the hole in your ★ .
How many boats go through the ★ every day?
Would you like to have a ★ at my new bike?
Have your read that ★ about California?
Dad's curry is delicious – he can ★ really well!

New words ▸ p. 50

What do you do if you're sad and ____________ ?	Was tut man, wenn man traurig und **deprimiert** ist?
Cold grey winter days are often ____________ .	Kalte, graue Wintertage können **deprimierend** sein.
He feels ______________ because he hurt her.	Er fühlt sich **schuldig**, weil er sie verletzt hat.
The murderer spent 20 years in ____________ .	Der Mörder verbrachte 20 Jahre im **Gefängnis**.
He lost two teeth in a ______________ .	Er hat in einer **Schlägerei** zwei Zähne verloren.
After the accident his life ______________ .	Nach dem Unfall **veränderte sich** sein Leben.
They didn't come, so I ______________ waiting.	Sie kamen nicht, also **gab** ich das Warten **auf**.
Sue is kissing to Jake, her new ________________ .	Sue küsst Jake, ihren neuen **Freund**.
Sam is dancing with his ______________ Jane.	Sam tanzt mit seiner **Freundin** Jane.
You'll like him when you _________________ him.	Du wirst ihn mögen, wenn du ihn **kennenlernst**.
This is ______________ , so please don't laugh.	Die Sache ist **ernst**, also bitte nicht lachen.

13 Crossword

Across

1 more than half the people in a group (8)
5 line between two countries (6)
9 very large sea (5)
10 be successful (7)
11 a person who doesn't eat meat (10)
13 what somebody thinks about something (7)
14 the top man or woman in a US state (8)

Down

2 There are a lot of ____________ cities in the Ruhr area of Germany. (10)
3 You could find this around a garden. (5)
4 become different (6)
6 When did Columbus ____________ America? (8)
7 The ____________ of Berlin is about 3.5 million. (10)
8 not legal (7)
12 a drink made of grapes (4)

New words ▸ pp. 51–52

I often feel ______ because nothing happens here.	Ich bin oft **gelangweilt**, weil hier nichts passiert.
If you drink so much wine you'll get ______ .	Wenn du so viel Wein trinkst, wirst du **betrunken**.
He's too old for the job. It can't ______ .	Er ist zu alt für die Stelle. Das kann nicht **gutgehen**.
______ I was very tired, I went to bed early.	**Da** ich sehr müde war, ging ich früh schlafen.
My brother's daughter is my ______ .	Die Tochter meines Bruders ist meine **Nichte**.
My sister's son is my ______ .	Der Sohn meiner Schwester ist mein **Neffe**.
You'll get ______ if you eat chips all the time.	Du wirst **dick**, wenn du immer Pommes isst.
He's very ______ because he eats so little.	Er ist sehr **mager**, weil er so wenig isst.
He ______ me money, but I didn't take it.	Er hat mir Geld **angeboten**, aber ich nahm es nicht.
Only $4! That's a fantastic ______ !	Nur $4! Das ist ein fantastisches **Angebot**!
He climbed out of the bath and took a ______ .	Er stieg aus der Wanne und nahm ein **Handtuch**.
I just don't understand it. It's a ______ to me.	Ich verstehe es einfach nicht. Es ist mir ein **Rätsel**.
The main ______ in the film is a detective.	Die Haupt**figur** in dem Film ist ein Detektiv.
the famous ______ between Romeo and Juliet	die berühmte **Romanze** zwischen Romeo und Julia
______ can destroy love.	**Eifersucht** kann die Liebe zerstören.
Drugs are a big ______ problem.	Drogen sind ein großes **soziales** Problem.

14 The best word

Finde in jeder Schublade das Wort,
das am besten in die Lücke passt.

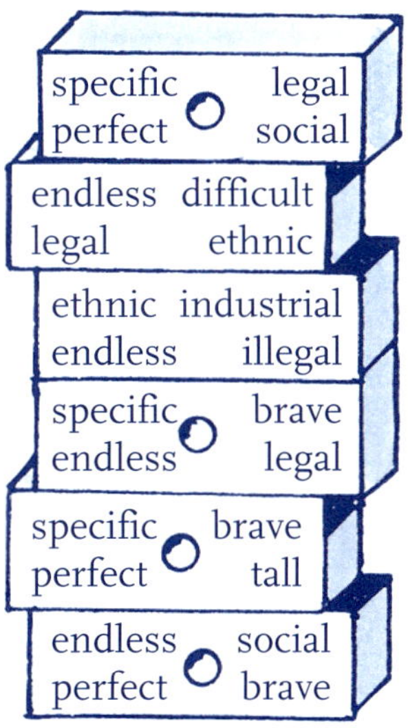

1 It's a ______ day for a picnic.

2 The presentation was so boring – it seemed ______ !

3 Bochum is an ______ city in the west of Germany.

4 Do you know if it's ______ to copy CDs?

5 If you have a ______ question, you can mail it to us.

6 Discrimination is a big ______ problem.

15 Words with different meanings

Finde in der Liste die passenden Wörter zu den Paaren 1–7.
Trage sie ein und unterstreiche die deutschen Entsprechungen.

1
a) Du solltest dich wie ein Erwachsener verhalten!
b) Man muss gut sein, um im Theater zu spielen.
____

2
a) Ich bin ziemlich gut in Mathe.
b) Sie ist eine hübsche Frau.
____

3
a) Diese Antwort ist richtig.
b) Gleich musst du rechts abbiegen.
right

4
a) Ich muss am nächsten Bahnhof umsteigen.
b) Bitte ändere die Überschrift auf Seite 2.
____

5
a) Versuch mal, die Antwort herauszufinden.
b) Keine Angst! Es wird gut ausgehen.
____

6
a) eine kleine Hütte
b) sehr wenig Zeit
____

7
a) Sie hat schon wieder eine Erkältung.
b) Ich will nicht hinaus in die Kälte.
____

act
change
cold
little
pretty
~~right~~
work out

14 Hour glasses

Übersetze die Wörter und trage sie in die passende Sanduhr ein.

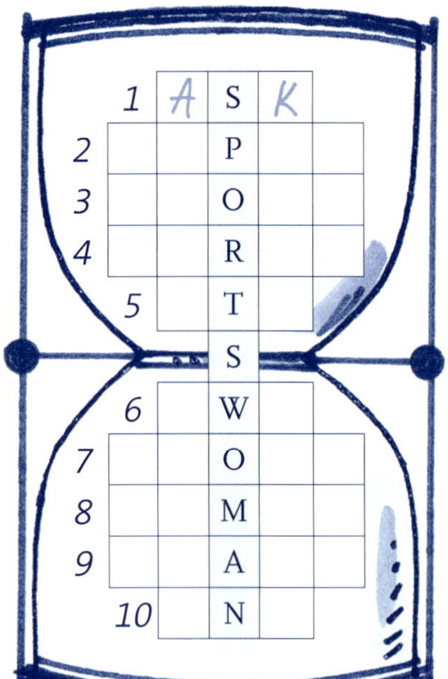

1 fragen – sich verhalten
2 Wohnblock – Thema
3 hell, blond – menschlich
4 anbieten – gelangweilt
5 aß – Zoo
6 eigene(r, s) – aß
7 zusammenstoßen – kurz
8 Frau – Hütte
9 sich ausruhen – Weintraube
10 beenden – wenige

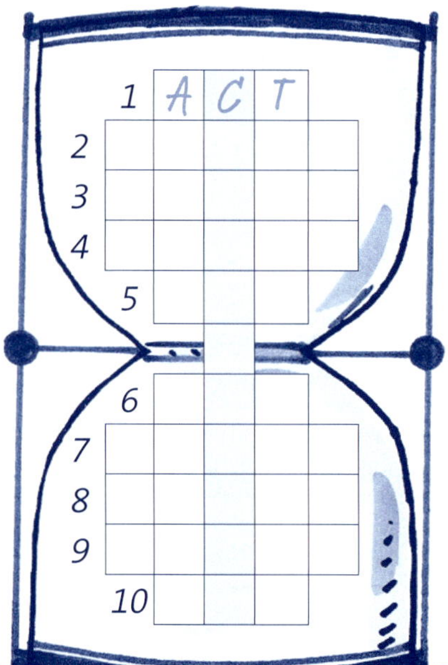

Das geheime Wort in der rechten Sanduhr heißt: Englisch ____________

Deutsch ____________

17 Lost words

Ergänze die Sätze mit den Wörtern rechts.

1 I don't really like his attitude to money.

2 Are people here prejudiced ___________ immigrants?

3 The children were hungry and begged ___________ food.

4 After two hours, firefighters succeeded ___________ putting the fire out.

5 Dad says he's going to give ___________ smoking.

6 The car crashed ___________ a stone wall.

7 It's illegal to discriminate ___________ women.

8 She fits ___________ very well – everyone in the group likes her.

9 Half ___________ the people in the US live on the coast.

10 In basketball, being tall gives you an advantage ___________ other players.

18 Word pairs

Welche Wörter passen zusammen?

Unit 3

New words ▸ pp. 54–55

Stop! The ______________________ is red.	Halt an! Die **Ampel** ist rot.
The school was __________ed in the 19th century.	Die Schule wurde im 19. Jahrhundert **gegründet**.
It's a _______________ to play tricks on 1st April.	Es ist **Tradition**, am 1. April Streiche zu spielen.
We don't know if he's __________ or dead.	Wir wissen nicht, ob er **am Leben** oder tot ist.
We drove out of the city into the _______________ .	Wir fuhren aus der Stadt hinaus aufs **Land**.
The town festival is a big _______________ here.	Das Stadtfest ist hier ein großes **Ereignis**.
I said nothing __________ , but then I spoke.	**Am Anfang** sagte ich nichts, aber dann sprach ich.

1 Word search

Finde im Rätsel 18 Begriffe zum Thema "family". Schreibe dann das Wort und die deutsche Übersetzung auf. (↓ →)

M	Y	C	J	I	G	O	D	Y	D	S	O	N
O	U	O	M	U	R	C	U	O	Y	S	H	I
T	X	U	D	T	A	D	F	G	W	I	F	E
H	U	S	B	A	N	D	P	C	S	T	V	C
E	F	I	T	T	D	X	Y	U	N	C	L	E
R	S	N	X	Y	P	T	J	G	T	H	B	H
O	Y	I	G	R	A	N	D	C	H	I	L	D
T	R	P	T	U	R	R	T	O	K	L	M	A
R	N	E	P	H	E	W	S	S	F	D	U	U
T	I	D	A	X	N	A	S	V	C	C	Q	G
W	A	B	R	O	T	H	E	R	Y	W	Q	H
I	I	R	E	V	S	P	G	H	A	U	N	T
N	I	B	N	E	B	J	C	Y	J	O	F	E
S	I	S	T	E	R	F	F	A	T	H	E	R
G	B	D	S	L	K	X	J	N	G	L	Q	O

mother – Mutter

____

____

____

____

____

____

____

____

____

____

____

____

____

____

____

____

____

2 Scrambled words: School

Die Buchstabenrätsel ergeben Wörter, die mit der Schule zu tun haben. Benutze sie, um die Sätze zu vervollständigen.

1	L A R S S O M O C	The students sat in the classroom and waited for the teacher.
2	R I S E V E	I'll have to ____________ geography before tomorrow's test.
3	C E X A H N E G	We have an ______________ student from France in our class this term.
4	P E X L A N I	If you don't understand something, ask the teacher to ______________ it.
5	C R O P T E J	We're doing a ______________ on the US in English this term.
6	S O L N E S	Our next ______________ is maths, and after that we have history.
7	S A S E Y	When do we have to hand in our history __________ ?
8	D A H E	Jake is in big trouble. He has to go and see the __________ teacher.
9	R E X I S E C E	Read the instructions well before you start the ______________ .
10	K O L O P U	Can you ____________ this word in an English dictionary?
11	R O B A D	It's harder to see the ____________ if you sit at the back of the classroom.
12	B J U S T E C	I like English a lot, but science is my favourite ________________ .

3 Last letter – first letter

Der letzte Buchstabe von jedem Wort ist gleichzeitig der erste des nächsten Wortes.

1 Jacke, Jackett
2 Turnschuhe
3 Sweatshirt
4 Oberteil
5 Schlafanzug
6 Hemd
7 Hose
8 kurze Hose
9 Rock
10 Strumpfhose
11 Socken
12 Schuhe

New words ▸ p. 56

Does Germany need a better school ___________ ?	Braucht Deutschland ein besseres Schul**system**?
Kids start ____________________ school at six.	Kinder fangen mit 6 Jahren in der **Grund**schule an.
______________ comes before elementary school.	Der **Kindergarten** kommt vor der Grundschule.
The American school year has two ___________ .	Das amerikanische Schuljahr hat zwei **Semester**.
Monday is 1st May, so I have a ______________	Montag ist der 1. Mai, also habe ich einen **Tag frei**.
___________ is the main festival in the church year.	**Ostern** is das Hauptfest des Kirchenjahres.
US school students eat lunch in the ___________ .	US-Schüler essen zu Mittag in der **Schulkantine**.
An A is the highest ______________ you can get.	Ein A ist die beste **Note**, die man bekommen kann.
Do we have Art or History next ______________ ?	Ist die nächste **Stunde** Kunst oder Geschichte?
Doing sport is good for your ______________ .	Sport zu treiben ist gut für die **Gesundheit**.
She wants to ______________ history after school.	Nach der Schule will sie Geschichte **studieren**.
We play basketball in the school ______________ .	Wir spielen Basketball in der Schulturn**halle**.
read announcements on the ___________________	Bekanntgaben am **Schwarzen Brett** lesen
The ___________________ says what you can wear.	Die **Kleiderordnung** sagt, was man tragen darf.
The money fell through a ________ in my pocket.	Das Geld fiel durch ein **Loch** in meiner Tasche.
Will dictionaries ___________________ in the test?	Werden Wörterbücher im Test **erlaubt** sein?
The glass fell onto the ground and ______________ .	Das Glas fiel zu Boden und ging **kaputt**.
Is the suit OK or do I need to ______________ ?	Ist der Anzug OK, oder muss ich mich **umziehen**?

4 Verb forms

Ergänze die Tabelle der unregelmäßigen Verben.

1	make	made	made
2	begin		
3			torn
4		studied	
5		cried	

6		shook	
7		took	
8			kept
9		ran	
10	break		

5 The fourth word

Welches Wort fehlt hier?

1	boy – boys	man – men	*6*	students – student	children – ______
2	hand – hands	foot – ______	*7*	eyes – eye	teeth – ______
3	robber – robbers	thief – ______	*8*	husbands – husband	wives – ______
4	fox – foxes	wolf – ______	*9*	hamsters – hamster	mice – ______
5	tomato – tomatoes	potato – ______	*10*	tests – test	quizzes – ______

6 Hidden words

Ergänze die Wortgruppen, indem du Wörter mit Buchstaben des Wortes „kindergarten" bildest.

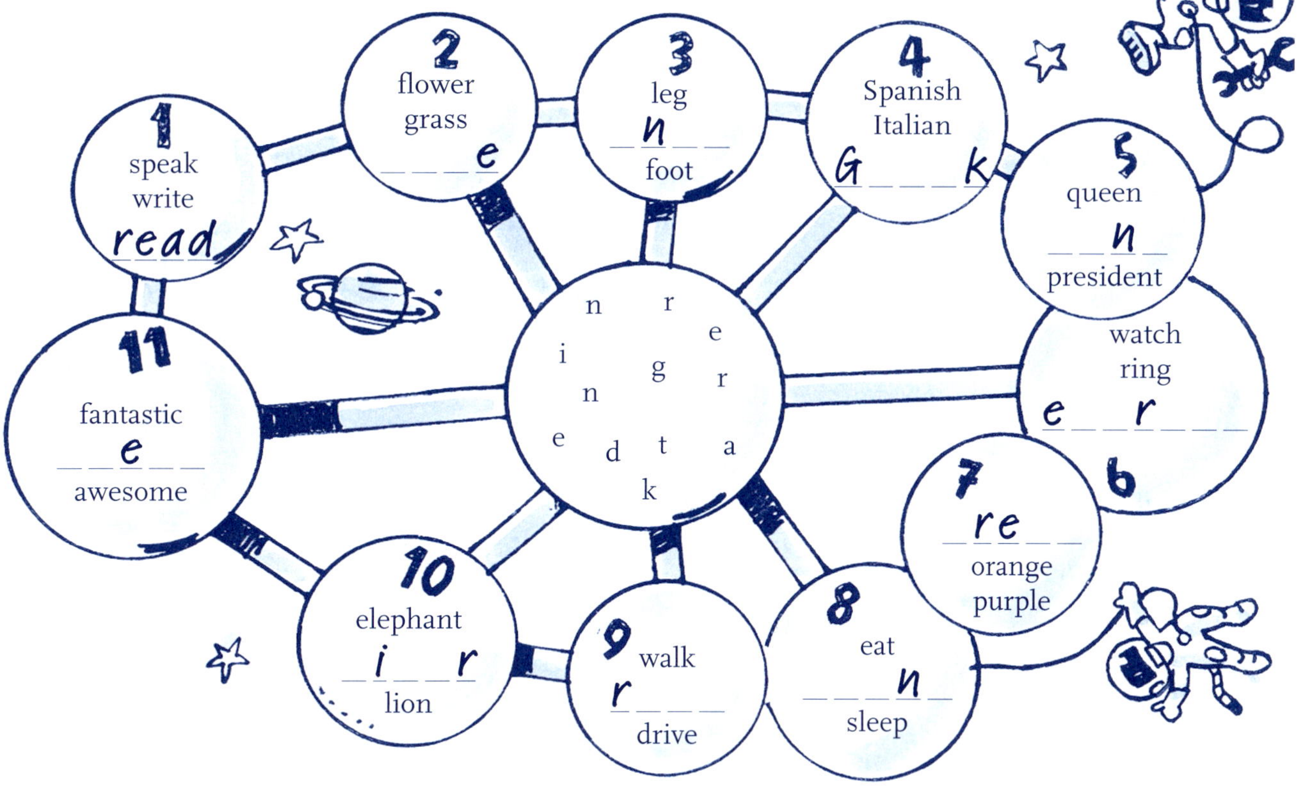

7 What are the words?

Wie übersetzt man das Wort ***change*** *ins Deutsche?*

1 Grandma never **changes**. She's as beautiful as ever. ______

2 We still have to **change** our pounds into dollars. ______

3 You don't have to **change** – those jeans are fine. ______

4 We have to **change** at Waterloo Station. ______

5 I'd like to **change** to a room with a view of the sea. ______

New words ▸ pp. 57–58

What time is the ______________ with the boss?	Wann findet die **Besprechung** mit dem Chef statt?
products like butter, milk, yoghurt ______________	Produkte wie Butter, Milch, Jogurt **und so weiter**
Too few people ______________________ in politics.	Zu wenig Menschen **engagieren sich** in der Politik.
French is my favourite ______________ language.	Französisch ist meine Lieblings**fremd**sprache.
We should ________ the arguments of both sides.	Man soll die Argumente beider Seiten **debattieren**.
I have a French ______________ after the break.	Nach der Pause habe ich Französisch**unterricht**.
Tourists in Egypt often go to see the ___________ .	Touristen in Ägypten besuchen oft die **Pyramiden**.
___________ usually has more sugar than juice.	**Limonade** enthält meistens mehr Zucker als Saft.
I eat chicken, turkey and other kinds of ________ .	Ich esse Hähnchen, Pute und andere **Geflügel**arten.
I like chocolate with fruit or ______________ .	Ich mag Schokolade mit Früchten oder **Nüssen**.
We had lamb with green ___________ for lunch.	Wir aßen Lamm mit grünen **Bohnen** zu Mittag.
_____________ bread is healthier than white bread.	**Vollkorn**brot ist gesünder als Weißbrot.
____________ is important so that you don't get fat.	**Bewegung** ist wichtig, damit man nicht dick wird.
Is _______ for breakfast healthier than cornflakes?	Ist **Müsli** zum Frühstück gesünder als Cornflakes?
Let's go for a walk in the ___________ air.	Lass uns an der **frischen** Luft spazieren gehen.

8 Spot the mistakes

In jedem Satz sind zwei Fehler.
Unterstreiche und korrigiere sie.

1. After school my older brother want to studie geography.   want ______________ ______________
2. You usually get reis with your meel at a Chinese restaurant. ______________ ______________
3. We spent the hole afternoon at a meating. ______________ ______________
4. Water came in through the whole in my schuh. ______________ ______________
5. If you brake the rules, you'll be in troble. ______________ ______________
6. We had a good debatte in history klass today. ______________ ______________
7. Get more exersise, and spend more time in the frish air. ______________ ______________
8. I love to travel to forein countrys. ______________ ______________

9 Pronunciation

Ordne die Wörter aus der Box der richtigen Aussprachegruppe zu.

aɪ ɪ iː

al*i*ve bullet*i*n countrys*i*de eng*i*ne exerc*i*se
f*i*ght k*i*lo k*i*ndergarten l*i*ght mach*i*ne
magaz*i*ne meet*i*ng p*i*zza pol*i*ce sk*i*
s*i*ck trad*i*tion w*i*ne

fight	sick	magazine

10 Lost words

Ergänze die Sätze mit den Wörtern rechts.

1. If you take this train, you'll have to change _at_ Cologne.
2. Most students want to take part ______ the trip to Berlin.
3. I was nervous ______ first, but then I started to relax.
4. I'm good ______ languages, but not ______ maths.
5. Can you give me some change ______ the ticket machine, please?
6. Why don't you get involved ______ your local youth club?
7. Please be quiet! I have to study ______ the English test tomorrow.
8. Where did you get that information ______ the wine industry?
9. How much time a week do you spend ______ your hobbies?

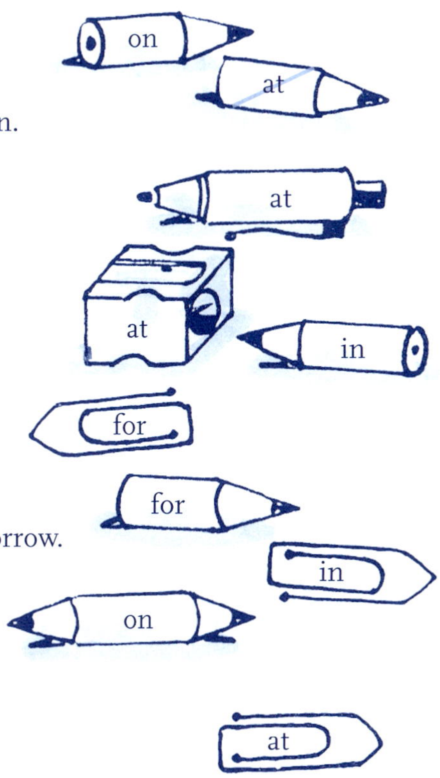

New words ▸ p. 59

We like to eat ________ fruit, not fruit from far away.	Wir essen gerne Obst **vom Ort**, nicht von weit weg.
Bad Arolsen is Hermann's ____________________ .	Bad Arolsen ist Hermanns **Partnerstadt**.
I'm ____________ . Maybe there's been an accident.	Ich bin **besorgt**. Vielleicht gab es einen Unfall.
_______________ is different from American football.	**Fußball** ist anders als American Football.
He's not _________ enough. He needs exercise.	Er ist nicht **aktiv** genug. Er braucht Bewegung.

11 More about ...
German immigrants in North America

Vervollständige den Text mit den Wörtern aus der Box.

as escape families first
in Jewish millions
newspapers number went

Since the 17th century, _______________ (1) of Germans have left Europe to make new homes in North America. 1683 is an important date. In that year, in Pennsylvania, 13 families founded the _______________ (2) German town in the New World: they called it Germantown. In 1750, about 45,000 Germans were already living in Pennsylvania alone. During the next century, the _______________ (3) of immigrants grew all the time. One reason why they went to America was

that they wanted a freer life. Over a million people _______________ (4) to the US after the revolution of 1848 *failed. In the 19th century, New York City was popular with German immigrants. Over 100,000 Germans were living there _______________ (5) 1860. And there were 50 German schools, 20 churches, at least 10 bookshops and two German language daily _______________ (6). In the 1930s there were many _______________ (7) immigrants, who had to leave Germany to _______________ (8) from the Nazis. One of them was Albert Einstein. After World War II, Germans still went to the US, but the numbers weren't _______________ (9) high as before. Today about 58 million Americans say that their _______________ (10) once came from Germany.

fail= scheitern

New words ▸ pp. 62–65

Hope to see you soon, ________ Peter	Ich hoffe, wir sehen uns bald. **Alles Gute**, Peter
Would you like to ________ the postcard to Jake?	Willst du die Postskarte an Jake **unterschreiben**?
The ________ age in my class is 14.	Das **Durchschnitts**alter in meiner Klasse ist 14.
How big is England? – 130,000 ________ .	Wie groß ist England? – 130.000 **Quadratkilometer.**
It's very cold – about ________ 15 degrees.	Es ist sehr kalt – etwa **minus** 15 Grad.
Yesterday it was minus 2 degrees; today it's ____ 2.	Gestern hatten wir minus 2 Grad; heute **plus** 2.
In Europe temperatures are in ________ .	In Europa sind Temperaturen in **Celsius**.
Have you got any ________ on the subject?	Hast du ein paar **Gedanken** zum Thema?
There's music to download ________ .	**Im Internet** gibt es Musik zum Herunterladen.
This bed's too ________ : I prefer hard beds.	Das Bett is zu **weich**: Mir sind harte Betten lieber.
There's no alcohol in a ________ .	In einem **alkoholfreien Getränk** ist kein Alkohol.
He gave me a few very ________ tips.	Er gab mir ein paar sehr **nützliche** Tipps.
There are over 500 ________ in 100 g chocolate.	Es sind über 500 **Kalorien** in 100 g Schokolade.
How much sugar does 100 g chocolate ________ ?	Wieviel Zucker **enthalten** 100 g Schokolade?

12 Definitions

Vervollständige die Definitionen mit Wörtern aus der linken Sprühwolke. Trage die Lösungen aus der anderen Sprühwolke in die rechte Spalte ein.

1	a kind of school for children ________ 4 and 6 years	kindergarten
2	You use this word for a person or ________ from another ________ .	________
3	when people ________ together to discuss or ________ something	________
4	________ you can do at school when ________ are over	________
5	________ off your clothes and put on ________ ones	________

New words ▸ p. 67

__________ the story in about 100 words.	**Fasse** die Geschichte in 100 Wörtern **zusammen**.
I only read a __________ of the report.	Ich las nur eine **Zusammenfassung** des Berichts.
The ______ will do a tour of the city with us.	Der **Fremdenführer** macht mit uns eine Stadttour.
Shall we go by ______ or by canoe?	Sollen wir mit **Schlauchboot** oder Kanu fahren?
Do you like the new _______ of the old song?	Magst du die neue **Version** von dem alten Lied?
This is a copy. The _________ is in London.	Dies ist eine Kopie. Das **Original** ist in London.
I prefer the new version to the _________ one.	Ich ziehe die neue Version der **ursprünglichen** vor.
If you ______ the sugar ___ , it will be less sweet.	Wenn du Zucker **weglässt**, wird es weniger süß.

13 Word ladder

Gehe von unten nach oben, indem du auf jeder Sprosse einen Buchstaben veränderst.

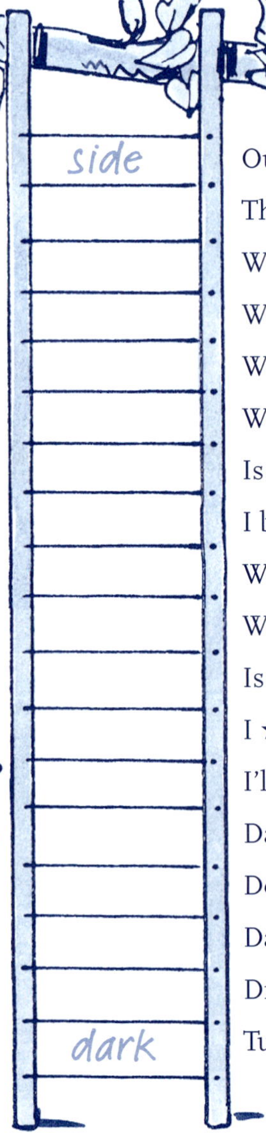

Our flat is on the sunny ★ of the street.
The bank robbers looked for a place to ★ their money.
Where can I learn to ★ a horse?
Would you like ★ or potatoes with the stew?
Why doesn't our cat catch ★ ?
We still have to walk another ★ .
Is the rabbit ★ or female?
I bought this sweatshirt in the summer ★.
Why does Jake tell the ★ jokes all the time?
Would you like ★ tea?
Is your arm still ★ ? – Yes, it still hurts a bit.
I ★ this dress for the first time yesterday.
I'll have to look this ★ up in the dictionary.
Dad starts ★ at 8 am every morning.
Do you sell ★ sausages?
Dad has left the car in the car ★ .
Did you get a good ★ in the test?
Turn on the reading lamp – it's getting ★ .

New words ▸ *p. 68*

Is there a __________ that we can meet?	Gibt es eine **Möglichkeit**, dass wir uns treffen?
Do you want to __________ the DVD for this cap?	Willst du die DVD gegen diese Mütze **tauschen**?
We __________ a new parliament every 5 years.	Wir **wählen** alle 5 Jahre ein neues Parlament.
Which party won the ______________ ?	Welche Partei hat die **Wahl** gewonnen?
Would you __________ for or against this law?	Würdest du für oder gegen dieses Gesetz **stimmen**?
They ______________ and married soon after.	Sie **verliebten sich** und heirateten bald danach.
My back ________ again. I'll have to see a doctor.	Mein Rücken **tut** wieder **weh**. Ich muss zum Arzt.
If you have toothache, go to the ____________ .	Wenn du Zahnschmerzen hast, geh zum **Zahnarzt**.
They were ______________ with fear.	Sie **schwitzten** vor Furcht.

14 Word friends

In jedem Haus gibt es drei Wörter bzw. Wortverbindungen, die man direkt nach dem Verb auf der Fahne benutzen kann. Unterstreiche sie.

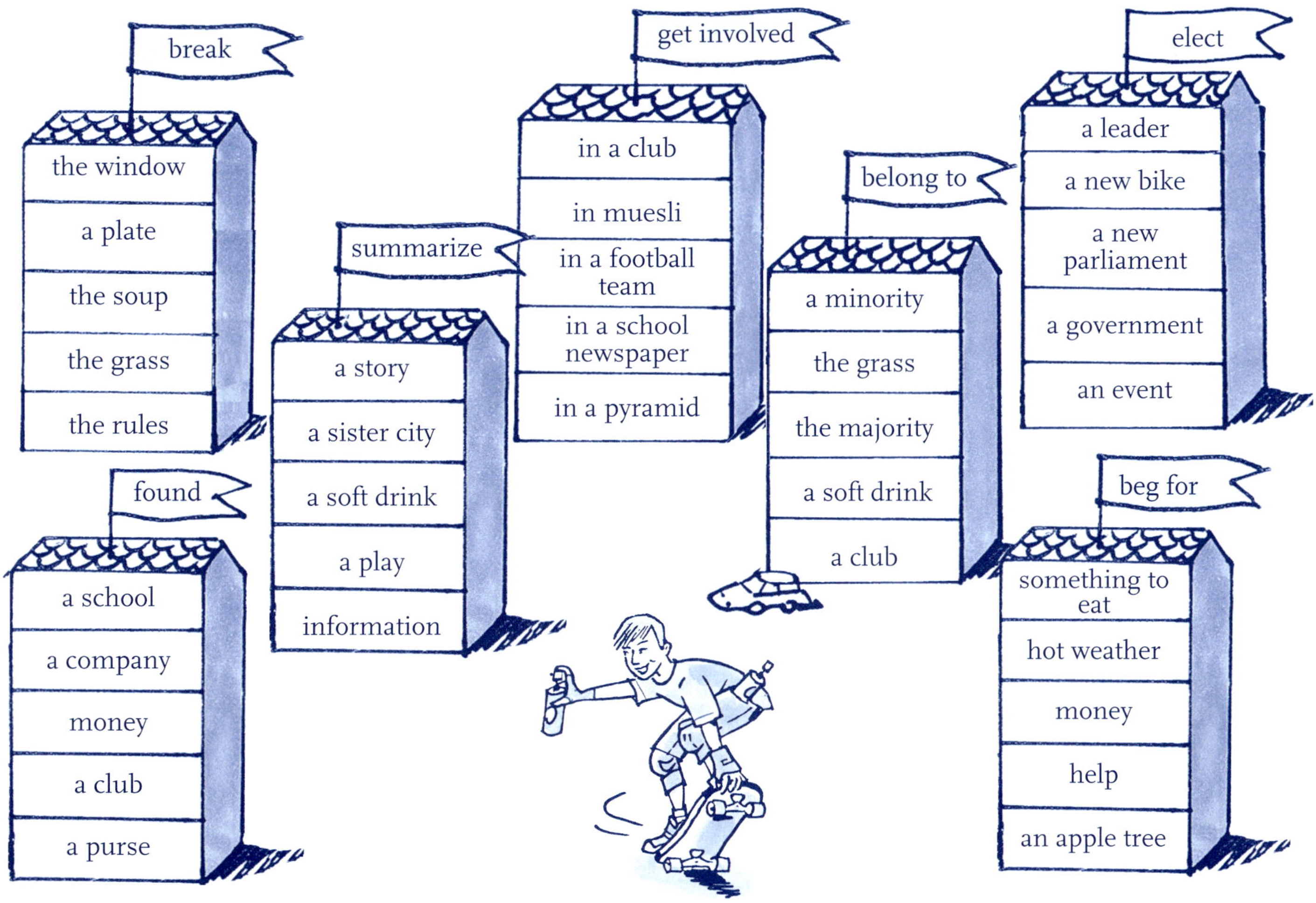

New words ▸ pp. 69–70

When you shop, you should ________ prices.	Beim Einkaufen solltest du die Preise **vergleichen**.
It's cold. – ________ . I'll wear my coat.	Es ist kalt. – **Ist egal.** Ich ziehe meinen Mantel an.
You often go red if you're ____________ .	Man wird oft rot, wenn man **verlegen** ist.
The ________ went up and the show started.	Der **Vorhang** ging auf, und die Show begann.
His dog follows him like a ____________ .	Sein Hund folgt ihm wie ein **Schatten**.
Do people go to __________ when they die?	Kommt man in den **Himmel**, wenn man stirbt?
I felt sick, and I had to ______________ .	Mir war schlecht, und ich musste **mich übergeben**.
She's pretty. And ________ she's clever too.	Sie ist hübsch. Und **nebenbei bemerkt** auch klug.
These shoes hurt – they're much too ______ !	Diese Schuhe tun weh – sie sind viel zu **eng**!
If you ____ me a ________ , I'll help you too.	Wenn du mir einen **Gefallen tust**, helfe ich dir auch.
All the band's fans ________ and cheered.	Alle Fans der Band **klatschten** und jubelten.
He's so rude! Can't he be more __________ ?	Er ist so unhöflich! Kann er nicht **höflich**er sein?
Big crowds __________ against the new law.	Große Mengen **protestierten** gegen das neue Gesetz.
We sat in a __________ round the table.	Wir saßen im **Kreis** um den Tisch.
Boxers fight with their __________ .	Boxer kämpfen mit ihren **Fäusten**.
The film had a really exciting __________ .	Der Film hatte eine sehr spannende **Handlung**.

15 Word building

Vervollständige die englischen Begriffe mit Wörtern aus der Box.

~~boy~~ dress girl fire home ~~sister~~ sparkling sports ticket traffic

1 Freund – boy friend	*6* Partnerstadt – sister city
2 Freundin – ______________ friend	*7* Heimatstadt – ______________ town
3 Kleiderordnung – ______________ code	*8* Ampel – ______________ light
4 Sportlerin – ______________ woman	*9* Fahrkartenschalter – ______________ office
5 Sprudel – ______________ water	*10* Feuerwehrmann – frau ______________ fighter

16 Number crossword

Gleiche Zahlen sind gleiche Buchstaben. Die angegebenen Lösungen helfen dir, das gesamte Rätsel zu lösen.

Wo im Rätsel findet man das englische Wort für …

Wein	i down
Besprechung	
Regierung	
Turnhalle	
Ereignis	
Tradition	
Kreis	
ausgezeichnet	
Weintraube	
Gesundheit	
(jn.) wählen	
Protest	

17 Hour glasses

Übersetze die Wörter und trage sie in die passende Sanduhr ein.

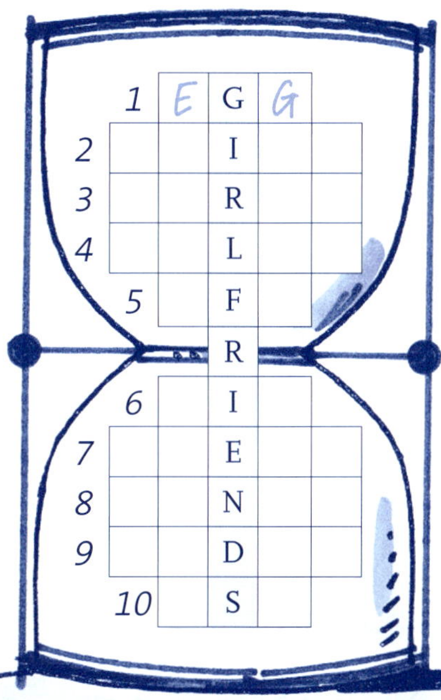

1 Eis – Ei
2 Reiseleiter/in – andere(r, s)
3 wählen – Erde
4 albern – frisch
5 ausgeschaltet – probieren
6 lassen – liegen
7 Schulnote – schwitzen
8 Zaun – Video
9 Ereignis – heute
10 verwenden – weinen

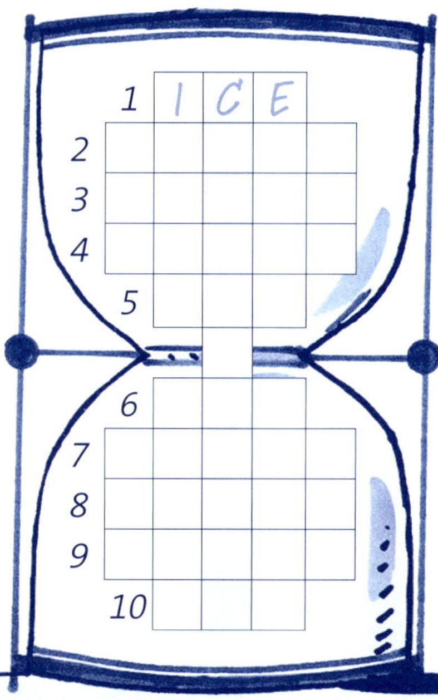

Das geheime Wort heißt: Englisch ____________________

Deutsch ____________________

Unit 4

New words ▸ *p. 76*

If oil prices ________ , petrol will cost more.	Wenn die Ölpreise **steigen**, wird Benzin teurer.
I fell asleep __________ the film.	Ich bin **während** des Films eingeschlafen.
The American _______________ began in 1861.	Der amerikanische **Bürgerkrieg** begann 1861.
Millions were killed in the Second World ________ .	Millionen wurden im Zweiten Welt**krieg** getötet.
This summer shirt is made of 100% __________ .	Dieses Sommerhemd ist aus 100% **Baumwolle.**
Cotton was grown on big ____________________ .	Baumwolle wurde auf großen **Plantagen** angebaut.
There's a lot of crime and ____________ on TV.	Im TV gibt es viel Verbrechen und **Gewalt.**
She was the victim of a ____________ attack.	Sie war das Opfer eines **gewalttätigen** Angriffs.
I like __________________ films, without blood.	Ich mag **gewaltfreie** Filme, ohne Blut.
The logo of the ____________________ is 5 rings.	Das Logo der **Olympischen Spiele** sind 5 Ringe.

1 Word groups: Sports

Trage die Wörter aus der Box in die richtigen Listen ein.

canoeing champion cheerleader climbing
coach court footballer goalkeeper hiking
hunting ice rink pitch pool riding
runner running track skating ski slope
skiing stadium supporter

people

champion
____
____
____
____
____
____

places

____
____
____
____
____
____
____

activities

____
____
____
____
____
____
____

New words ▸ p. 77

Obama is the first ________________ president.	Obama ist der erste **afro-amerikanische** Präsident.
The ____________ leads the city government.	Der **Bürgermeister** führt die Stadtregierung.
be member of the ______________ movement	ein Mitglied der **Bürgerrechts**bewegung sein
We have the ____________ to speak freely.	Wir haben das **Recht** frei zu sprechen.
CNN is a big American TV ____________ .	CNN ist ein großer amerikanischer TV-**Sender**.

2 Word ladder

Gehe von unten nach oben, indem du auf jeder Sprosse einen Buchstaben veränderst.

Would you like to go out or stay at ★ this evening?
He fell into a big ★ and disappeared.
He plays an important ★ in the government.
Smoke from the burning house ★ into the sky.
How much money did you ★ ?
We played quite well, but we ★ the match.
Hurry, or we won't get the ★ bus.
You can really run very ★ !
She hit me in the face with her ★ .
Here's the ★ of people who are coming to my party.
Use the stairs – it's healthier than taking the ★.
He has a hard ★ , but he never seems to be unhappy.
We've met Mr Jones, but we don't know his ★ yet.
There's some white ★ in the fridge.
Can you sign your name on this ★, please?
Turn left into the little ★ after the post office.
If you're ★, the plane will leave without you.
Your flight leaves from ★ B27.
Would you like to play a ★ of cards?
It's boring to do the ★ things every day.
Would you like ★ milk in your tea?
Your eyes look red – are they ★ ?
Are you ★ that you remembered to close the window?
We can ★ the internet to get information for the project.

New words ▸ p. 78

look for a good film in the ______________	einen guten Film im **Fernsehprogramm** suchen
________ on TV is between 7 pm and 11 pm.	Die **Hauptsendezeit** im Fernsehen ist von 19 bis 23 Uhr.
He needs a plug and ________ for the lamp.	Er braucht einen Stecker und ein **Kabel** für die Lampe.
What a nice film! Is there a __________ ?	So ein schöner Film! Gibt's eine **Wiederholung**?
Everyone found the __________ very funny.	Alle fanden die **Komödie** sehr witzig.
______________ are films about real events.	**Dokumentarfilme** sind Filme über reale Ereignisse.
The new ________ is about love and death.	Im neuen **Fernsehspiel** geht's um Liebe und Tod.
Who plays the detective in the __________ ?	Wer spielt den Detektiv in der **Krimiserie**?
It's a __________ to kill somebody.	Es ist ein **Verbrechen**, jemanden zu töten.
a ______________ to find the best cook	ein **Wettbewerb**, um den besten Koch zu finden
__________ is a really terrible crime.	**Mord** ist ein wirklich furchtbares Verbrechen.
Dad's favourite ______________ is the news.	Die Nachrichten sind Papas Lieblings**sendung**.
Which music _____________ do you like?	Welchen Musik**kanal** magst du?
A _____________ reads the news.	Ein **Nachrichtensprecher** spricht die Nachrichten.
Over 13 million __________ saw the show.	Über 13 Millionen **Zuschauer** sahen die Show.
There __ nothing good __ at the cinema today.	Es **läuft** nichts Gutes im Kino heute.
The film is long – it __________ three hours.	Der Film ist lang – er **dauert** drei Stunden.

3 Spot the mistakes

In jedem Satz sind zwei Fehler. Unterstreiche und korrigiere sie.

1 You can watch lots of chanels on cabel TV. channels ____________ ____________

2 There's a good crimi serie on TV at the moment. ____________ ____________

3 Or we can watch the repeet of my favourite comedie. ____________ ____________

4 There's also a dokumentary about Afrikan-Americans. ____________ ____________

5 The poeple of Atlanta have chosen a new major. ____________ ____________

6 How many people were killed durring the zivil war? ____________ ____________

7 How many kandidates are their in the election? ____________ ____________

New words ▸ p. 79

That's ______________ . It can't be true.	Das ist **unglaublich**. Es kann nicht wahr sein.
There's always a ______________ at rush hour.	In der Hauptverkehrszeit gibt es immer einen **Stau**.
I waited ________ 20 minutes. Then I left.	Ich wartete 20 Minuten **lang**. Dann ging ich weg.
No, that's wrong! Do it ____________ .	Nein, das ist falsch. Mach's **so**.
The house was destroyed by a gas __________ .	Das Haus wurde durch eine Gas**explosion** zerstört.
Three policemen were killed by __________ .	Drei Polizisten wurden von **Terroristen** getötet.
I'll drive you to the ferry and _____ you ____ there.	Ich fahre dich zur Fähre und **setze** dich dort **ab**.
________ has he lived in Atlanta? – For 17 years.	**Seit wann** lebt er in Atlanta? – Seit 17 Jahren.

4 Word pairs

Welche Wörter passen zusammen?

New words ▸ p. 80

We had to stay at home ______________ the rain.	Wir mussten **wegen** des Regens zu Hause bleiben.
______________ nobody was hurt in the accident.	**Zum Glück** wurde niemand bei dem Unfall verletzt.
The police already know the ________ of the fire.	Die Polizei kennt schon die **Ursache** des Brandes.
Drive slowly or you'll ________ an accident.	Fahr langsam oder du wirst einen Unfall **verursachen**.
We've been here for 30 minutes, ________ 8:30.	Wir sind seit 30 Minuten hier, **seit** 8:30.
He wants a job, but hasn't found one ________ .	Er sucht Arbeit, hat aber **bis jetzt** keine gefunden.
He's ____________________ with his bad grades.	Er ist von seinen schlechten Noten **enttäuscht**.
We'll _______________ our fans if we lose.	Wir **enttäuschen** unsere Fans, wenn wir verlieren.
The painting is ______________ in the museum.	Das Gemälde ist im Museum **ausgestellt**.
Today is the first _________________ of his death.	Heute ist der erste **Jahrestag** seines Todes.
Many people believe in life after ___________ .	Viele Leute glauben an ein Leben nach dem **Tod**.
I'm ______________ ! You can paint really well.	Ich bin **beeindruckt**! Du kannst echt gut malen.
I can do the photo research in the ___________ .	Ich kann die Fotorecherche im **Archiv** machen.

5 The best word

Finde in jeder Schublade das Wort, das am besten in die Lücke passt.

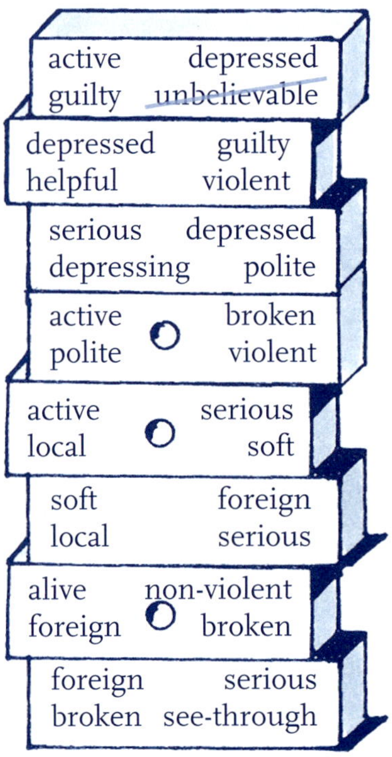

1. I've never seen anything like it before! It's unbelievable .
2. He was found _______________ of murder and sent to jail for 20 years.
3. Jake was very ____________________ when he didn't pass the exam.
4. If you're __________ , most people will be happy to help if you ask.
5. Sue's very _______________ in a charity that helps homeless teens.
6. Kim's writing an article for our _______________ newspaper.
7. It's _______________ , so you'll have to buy a new one.
8. If you speak a _______________ language, you can get a job abroad.

6 More about ... The Atlanta Olympics

Vervollständige den Text mit den Wörtern aus der Box.

anniversary
be
built
crowd
dollars
for
from
over
special
were

'And the winner is ... .' Six cities competed to be *host city to the 1996 Olympics: Athens, Atlanta, Belgrade, Manchester, Melbourne and Toronto. Many people expected that Melbourne or Toronto would __________ (1) chosen. But after the final round of voting, the winner was Atlanta. This success was very __________ (2), because 1996 was the 100th ______________ (3) of the modern Olympic Games.

Getting ready __________ (4) the Olympic Games always takes a long time. Atlanta needed six years to prepare, and the city spent billions of __________ (5). A new stadium and other sports venues were __________ (6). The city also built new streets and parks to make the centre more attractive. On 19th July 1996, the Games __________ (7) opened by President Clinton in front of a __________ (8) of 83,000 people. During the next seventeen days, over 10,000 athletes __________ (9) 197 nations took part in the Games. More than 2 million visitors came to Atlanta and about 3.5 billion people all ________ (10) the world followed the event on TV.

host city = Gastgeber; venue= Austragungsort

7 Opposites

Trage das Gegenteil der fett gedruckten Wörter in die Lücken ein.

1 Petrol prices have **fallen** / risen again.

2 We lived **together** / __________ for many years.

3 It's a question of **life** and __________ .

4 a **believable**/ an ______________ story

5 She's always very **polite**/ _______ to everyone.

6 a **non-violent** / __________ protest

7 I find this bed a bit **hard** / __________ .

8 a temperature of two degrees **plus** / __________

9 Is it **safe** / ______________ to swim here?

10 Is it **legal** / ____________ to download this?

New words ▸ p. 81

Who's the ______________ at your church?	Wie heißt der **Pastor** an deiner Kirche?
Blacks were often ______________ from whites.	Schwarze wurden oft von den Weißen **getrennt**.
____________ in South Africa ended in 1994.	Die **Rassentrennung** in Südafrika endete 1994.
There was lots of ____________ against the war.	Es gab viel **Protest** gegen den Krieg.
The students are organizing a protest _______ .	Die Studenten organisieren einen Protest**marsch**.
About 200 _________ take part in the Olympics.	Etwa 200 **Nationen** nehmen an der Olympiade teil.
Don't _________ somebody by the car he drives.	**Beurteile** niemanden nach dem Auto, das er fährt.
A hat helps to protect your _______ from the sun.	Ein Hut hilft, die **Haut** vor der Sonne zu schüzten.
I wasn't bored, _______ a bit tired.	Ich war nicht gelangweilt, **sondern** etwas müde.
Yesterday he _____ his first_______ in parliament.	Gestern **hielt** er seine erste **Rede** im Parlament.
The library is a good place for _________ work.	Die Bibliothek ist ein guter Ort für **Recherche**arbeit.
Wind is an important ____________ of energy.	Der Wind ist eine wichtige Energie**quelle**.
A _________ finds information on the internet.	Eine **Suchmaschine** findet Infos im Internet.
The police _______ the house, but found nothing.	Die Polizei **durchsuchte** das Haus, fand aber nichts.

8 Last letter – first letter

Der letzte Buchstabe von jedem Wort ist gleichzeitig der erste des nächsten Wortes.

1 beeindruckt
2 Fernsehspiel
3 Archiv
4 Explosion
5 nahe
6 Recherche
7 verletzen
8 Terrorist
9 werfen
10 Krieg
11 (auf)steigen
12 Endung
13 Regierung

New words ▸ pp. 84–86

A _______________ is better then an old monitor.	Ein **Flachbildschirm** ist besser als ein alter Monitor.
Turn the TV off with the ___________ .	Schalt das TV mit der **Fernbedienung** aus.
I _____________________ . I never watch anything.	Ich **zappe**, ich gucke nie etwas.
How many TV channels can you ______________ ?	Wie viele TV-Kanäle könnt ihr **empfangen**?
With ______ you receive lots of TV channels.	Über **Satellit** empfängt man viele TV-Kanälen.
The music is too loud. Please _______ it _______ .	Die Musik ist zu laut. Bitte **stelle** sie **leiser**.
That's very loud. Please turn down the ________ .	Das ist sehr laut. Bitte stelle die **Lautstärke** leiser.
listen to arguments and ___________________	Argumente anhören und **Schlüsse ziehen**
The ________ time is 9.53 pm.	Die **genaue** Zeit ist 21:53.
He often _________________ terrible headaches.	Er **leidet** oft **an** schrecklichem Kopfweh.

9 Crossword

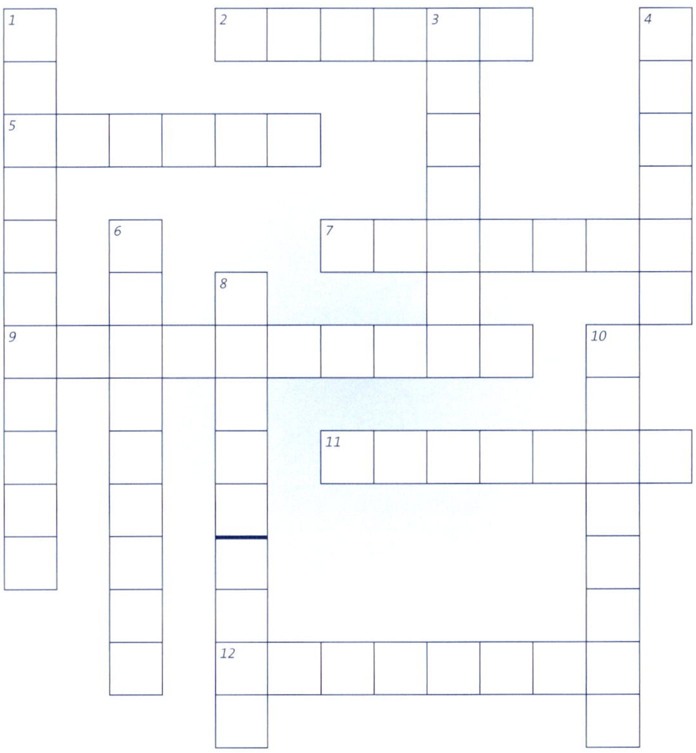

Across

2 You can see this again on TV. (6)
5 a show that makes you laugh (6)
7 a place where you can find information about the past (7)
9 the man or woman who reads the news on TV or radio (10)
11 make copies of a book, newspaper, etc. so that they can be sold (7)
12 It is usually published once a week or once a month and has pictures, stories and reports. (8)

Down

1 a TV film about real events or with information on a topic (11)
3 a report or other piece of writing in a newspaper (7)
4 word for a person who is watching TV (6)
6 It is usually published every day and has news, sports reports and other articles. (9)
8 time when the greatest number of viewers watch TV, usually in the evening (5, 4)
10 word for a person who is listening to the radio (8)

New words ▸ pp. 88–90

October 3rd is a ________ in Germany.	Der 3. Oktober ist ein **Feiertag** in Deutschland.
The US ________ lives in the White House.	Der US-**Präsident** wohnt im Weißen Haus.
I read a lot, ________ when I'm on holiday.	Ich lese viel, **besonders** wenn ich im Urlaub bin.
The ____ says what's legal or illegal.	Im **Gesetz** steht, was legal oder illegal ist.
It fell ________ like a house of cards.	Es fiel wie ein Kartenhaus **auseinander**.
If you print that, I'll take you to ________ .	Wenn Sie das drucken, bringe ich Sie vor **Gericht**.
Is there ____ in the living room for another sofa?	Gibt es **Platz** im Wohnzimmer für ein weiteres Sofa?
He acted ________ nothing had happened.	Er tat, **als ob** nichts geschehen wäre.
Help! I'm ________________ spiders.	Hilfe! Ich **habe schreckliche Angst vor** Spinnen.
If he gets worse, call a doctor ________ .	Wenn es ihm schlechter geht, ruf **sofort** den Arzt.
Did nobody ________ to help you?	Hat sich keiner **bereit erklärt**, dir zu helfen?
I need ________ to help with the project.	Ich brauche **Freiwillige**, die beim Projekt mithelfen.
There are 22 ________ to the next floor.	22 **Stufen** führen zum nächsten Stock.

10 Synonyms

Finde für jede Lücke zwei Synonyme.
Trage sie ein.

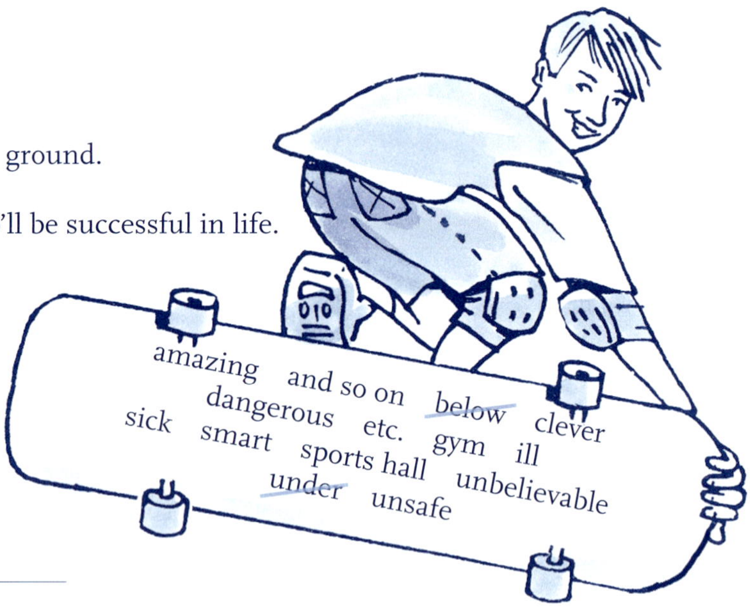

1 Moles live mostly below / under the ground.

2 She's a really ________ / ________ girl who'll be successful in life.

3 Be careful. That bridge looks a bit ________ / ________ .

4 Jake stayed at home because he felt ________ / ________ .

5 Does the ________ / ________ have a big pool?

6 That's ________ / ________ ! It can't be true.

7 We'll need pencils, pens, rubbers, ________ / ________ .

11 Odd word out

Ein Wort passt nicht. Finde und unterstreiche es.

1 crime – mayor – violence – war

2 comedy – crime series – documentary – network

3 cotton – jeans – shirt – top

4 bright – clean – dirty – tidy

5 afternoon – anniversary – morning – evening

6 excellent – explosion – fantastic – great

7 eating – drinking – during – sleeping

8 book – newsreader – comic – magazine

9 pavement – path – trail – queue

10 badminton – competition – football – tennis

11 governor – king – president – terrorist

12 car engine – search engine – train engine

13 exact – hair – skin – teeth

14 bus – car – lorry – traffic jam

12 Word search

Finde im Rätsel 18 Begriffe zum Thema "Politik und Gesellschaft". Schreibe jedes Wort und die deutsche Übersetzung auf. (↓ →)

I	M	S	R	C	E	X	B	N	K	W	V	T	S
P	A	R	L	I	A	M	E	N	T	E	O	D	M
D	Y	D	H	V	S	A	R	U	J	G	T	X	I
S	O	L	D	I	E	R	T	J	Q	U	E	E	N
F	R	B	M	L	P	C	L	N	K	D	E	R	O
C	V	P	M	R	Q	H	H	D	K	B	P	T	R
G	N	F	J	I	C	Y	U	I	I	X	R	X	I
O	B	R	I	G	O	V	E	R	N	M	E	N	T
V	M	E	S	H	K	X	H	X	G	V	S	N	Y
E	L	E	C	T	I	O	N	W	X	I	I	J	P
R	A	D	L	S	A	H	R	F	C	A	D	N	G
N	E	O	D	F	Y	C	P	R	O	T	E	S	T
O	B	M	R	H	N	L	P	J	U	U	N	Q	X
R	R	W	H	O	M	A	J	O	R	I	T	Y	T
S	F	C	K	E	T	W	C	N	T	T	B	G	R

parliament – Parlament

New words ▸ pp. 91–92

A ____________ often has to fight in wars.	Ein **Soldat** muss oft im Krieg kämpfen.
His eyes were hard and ____________ .	Seine Augen waren hart und **grausam**.
He's lonely. He ______________ stay with him.	Er ist einsam. Er **möchte, dass ich** bei ihm bleibe.
This is new for me. I'm doing it ____________ .	Das ist neu für mich. Ich mach es **zum ersten Mal**.
He's a great singer – his __________ is fantastic.	Er ist ein toller Sänger – seine **Stimme** ist fantastisch.
It's an old painting but it isn't very __________ .	Es is ein altes Gemälde, aber nicht sehr **wertvoll**.
Go to the doctor if you have a ______ in your leg.	Geh zum Arzt, wenn du **Schmerzen** im Bein hast.
The operation was __________ but successful.	Die Operation war **schmerzhaft** aber erfolgreich.
Water ____________ against the windscreen.	Wasser **spritzte** gegen die Windschutzscheibe.
A good ____________ prepares you for life.	Eine gute **Erziehung** bereitet auf das Leben vor.
What ____________ did our teacher study at?	An welcher **Universität** hat unser Lehrer studiert?
A ____________ writes articles in newspapers.	Ein **Journalist** schreibt Artikel in Zeitungen.
__________ are the titles of newspaper articles.	**Schlagzeilen** sind die Titel von Zeitungsartikeln.
find a ______________ for a text	eine **Überschrift** für einen Text finden

13 Hour glasses

Übersetze die Wörter und trage sie in die passende Sanduhr ein.

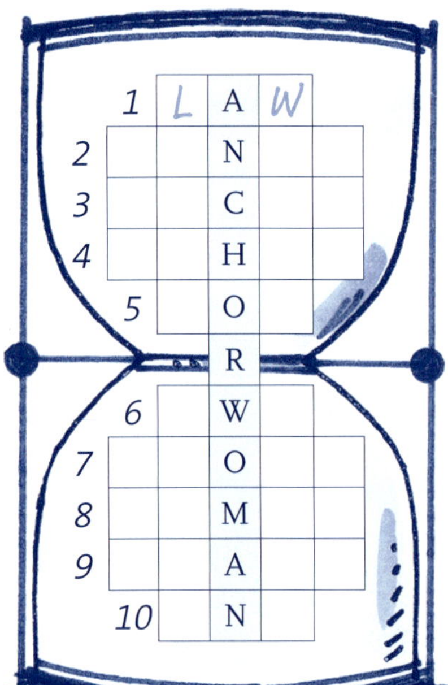

1 Sir – Gesetz
2 seit – Kamel
3 örtlich – menschlich
4 drücken – andere(r, s)
5 seit – hinzufügen
6 Krieg – eigene(r, s)
7 Motel – (Menschen)menge
8 Comic-Heft – brechen
9 Salat – auseinander
10 Sporthalle – beenden

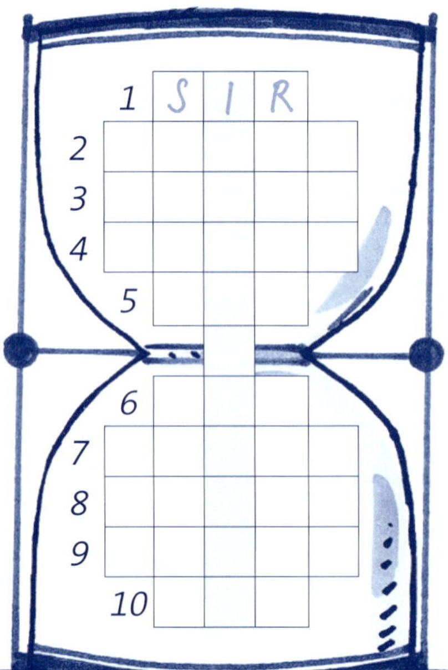

Das geheime Wort heißt: *Englisch* ______________________

Deutsch ______________________